Occasional Paper 18

Early Scholars' Visits to Central America

Reports by Karl Sapper, Walter Lehmann, and Franz Termer

❧

Translated by
Theodore E. Gutman

Edited by
Marilyn Beaudry-Corbett and Ellen T. Hardy

Cotsen Institute of Archaeology
University of California
Los Angeles, 2000

THE COTSEN INSTITUTE OF ARCHAEOLOGY AT UCLA
Richard M. Leventhal, Director
Marilyn Beaudry-Corbett, Director of Publications

EDITORS
Rita Demsetz, Marilyn Gatto, Beverly Godwin, Pat Hardwick, and Brenda Johnson-Grau

DESIGNER
Brenda Johnson-Grau

PRODUCTION
Amy Chen, Adam Cheng, Teresa González, Linda Tang, Michael Tang, and Alice Wang

Library of Congress Cataloging-in-Publication Data
Sapper, Karl, 1866-1945.
    Early scholars' visits to Central America : reports / by Karl Sapper, Walter Lehmann,
    and Franz Termer ; edited by Marilyn Beaudry-Corbett and Ellen T. Hardy ; translated
    by Theodore Gutman.
        p. cm. -- (Occasional paper ; 18)
    Includes bibliographical references.
    ISBN 0-917956-95-8
        1. Indians of Central America--Social life and customs. 2. Indians of Central
    America--Material culture. 3. Ethnology--Central America. 4. Central America--Social
    life and customs. 5. Central America--Description and travel. 6. Sapper, Karl,
    1866-1945--Journeys--Central America. 7. Lehman, Walter,
    1878-1939--Journeys--Central America. 8. Termer, Franz, 1894--Journeys--Central
    America. I. Lehmann, Walter, 1878-1939. II. Termer, Franz, 1894- III. Beaudry-Corbett,
    Marilyn. IV. Hardy, Ellen T. V. Title. VI. Occasional paper (University of California,
    Los Angeles. Institute of Archaeology) ; 18.

    F1434.2.S63 S36 2000
    972.8'00497--dc21   99-055214

Contents

Preface

THEODORE E. GUTMAN (1909–1997), the translator of the essays published in this volume, obtained his Doctor of Law degree from the State University of Jena, Germany, in 1932. Following his retirement from business in the early 1970s he became actively involved in various aspects of archaeology: participating in field projects in North America, Mexico, Guatemala, and Costa Rica; conducting laboratory analyses and library research; and translating scholarly works by early German researchers. After the publication of his translation of Karl Sapper's *The Verapaz in the Sixteenth and Seventeenth Centuries: A Contribution to the Historical Geography and Ethnography of Northeastern Guatemala* (1985), he continued working on various translation projects. The articles compiled here concentrate on regions and persons who had particular meaning for Ted.

THE TRANSLATIONS

Translations of scholarly work present a series of challenges beyond those of standard literary translation. When the length of time between writing and translating is as long as with these articles, even more challenges have to be met and Ted used his knowledge and experience to prepare as faithful translations as he could. Then we as editors set ourselves the goal of making available in an accessible manner the translated information from these early scholars. The purpose of this volume is not to engage in historical criticism. The critical analysis of historical sources is an important part of scholarship and several commentators touch upon that in their introductory sections.

We also decided to maintain the spirit but not the original style of the writers by presenting a more literal translation. The accuracy of the translations has been checked against the original articles by Charlotte Dugdale and we thank her and her keen eye for eliminating some inaccuracies.

The style of scholarly presentation in the fields of anthropology and archaeology has changed since these contributions were originally published and we have followed current conventions. The most obvious changes are explained here for the reader who may consult the originals.

BIBLIOGRAPHY

Citations have been placed within the text rather than in footnotes. The combined bibliography presents the complete set of references. For ethnohistoric sources, the version cited by the German author is included, along with volume and page numbers where given. The bibliography lists the cited version along with any more recent facsimile reprint that can be more easily consulted by the reader. In this compilation the *Handbook of Middle American Indians,* volumes 13 to 15 and supplement 4, were used as guides. We did not attempt to verify the page citations in the original publication nor to determine whether pagination in reprint editions is the same as in the version available to the scholars.

FOOTNOTES

Other than citations, the German author's footnotes are retained in the chapter. Editors' endnotes are used in a few instances where the scholar made an error or omission. The correct term is used in the text; an endnote gives the author's original term. In chapter 2, for example, Sapper incorrectly cited *ánum* as the Spanish term for soul. The correct term is *ánima* or *alma.* We have used the correct term in the text and added an endnote giving Sapper's original.

FIGURES

The illustrations are reproduced from the original publications. In one case, however, numbers have been added; in two cases, the figures have been renumbered for consistency and ease of reference. In all cases, callouts have been added.

ORTHOGRAPHY OF THE NATIVE LANGUAGES AND PLACE-NAMES

To make these writings most useful to the current research community we have had all words in different native languages reviewed by language specialists. Currently accepted orthography is used in the text. Each in-chapter glossary presents the current spelling along with that in the original publication, the English meaning, and a Spanish term where word equivalence exists.

In a few instances the spelling or presentation of place-names has changed. The first time the geographical location is mentioned the form used in the original is given along with the current form in parentheses; subsequently only the current spelling is used. An exception is chapter 5, Sapper's report on a visit to Honduras. The ethnic group then called Paya are now known as the Pech. Paya has been left in Sapper's text; commentators, however, use Pech.

Marilyn Beaudry-Corbett
Ellen T. Hardy

Acknowledgments

Many people provided expert information to help us ensure the overall accuracy of this publication. We thank them all for their assistance. Also, well-deserved thanks to the competent Publications Unit staff, coordinated and directed by Brenda Johnson-Grau, who produced the volume: Adam Cheng, Rita Demsetz, Marilyn Gatto, Beverly Godwin, Pat Hardwick, Teresa González, Linda Tang, Michael Tang, and Alice Wang.

GERMAN LANGUAGE

Charlotte Dugdale, Gutman Reading Room, Cotsen Institute of Archaeology at UCLA

NATIVE LANGUAGES

Adolfo Constenla Umaña, University of Costa Rica

Andrés Cuz Mucú, Past President, Academia de las Lenguas Mayas de Guatemala

Dennis Holt, Quinnipiac College, Hamden, Connecticut

Fernando Peñalosa, Yax Te' Foundation, Rancho Palos Verdes, California

SCIENTIFIC NAMES

Virginia Popper, Paleoethnobotany Laboratory, Cotsen Institute of Archaeology at UCLA

David Verity, Mildred Mathias Botanical Garden, University of California, Los Angeles

Thomas Wake, Zooarchaeology Laboratory, Cotsen Institute of Archaeology at UCLA

MAPS

Terisa Green, Digital Archaeology Laboratory, Cotsen Institute of Archaeology at UCLA

MARILYN BEAUDRY-CORBETT
ELLEN T. HARDY

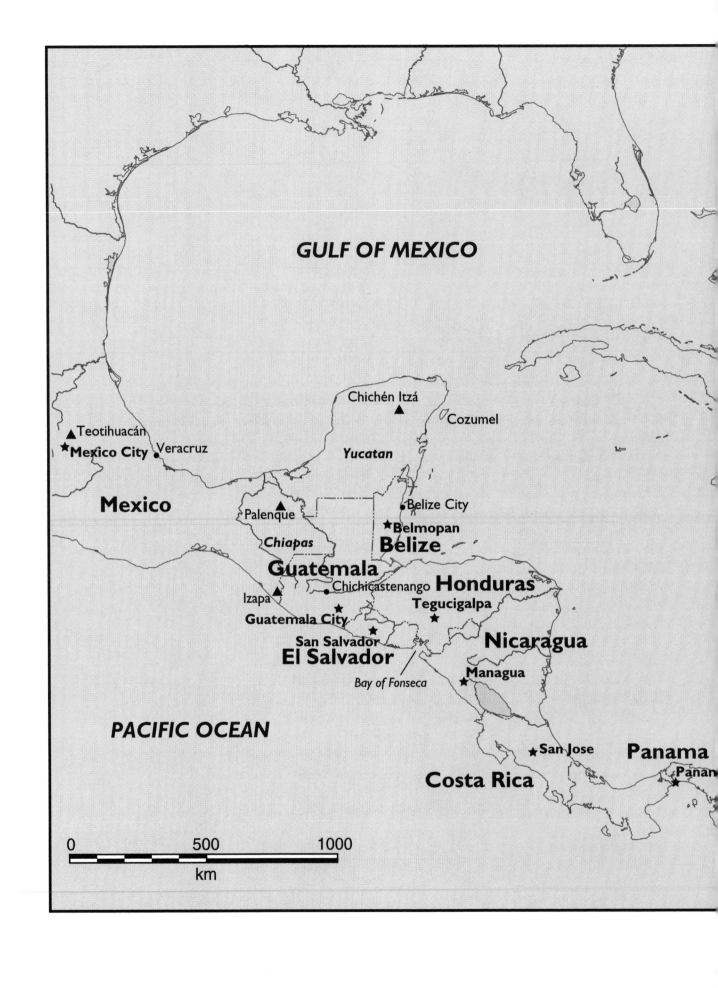

GULF OF MEXICO

Chichén Itzá ▲

Cozumel

▲ Teotihuacán

★ Mexico City Veracruz •

Yucatan

Mexico

Palenque ▲

• Belize City

Chiapas

★ Belmopan

Belize

Guatemala

Chichicastenango • Honduras

Izapa ▲

★ Tegucigalpa
★

★ Guatemala City

San Salvador ★ Nicaragua

El Salvador

Bay of Fonseca ★ Managua

PACIFIC OCEAN

★ San Jose Panama

Costa Rica Panan
★

0   500   1000

km

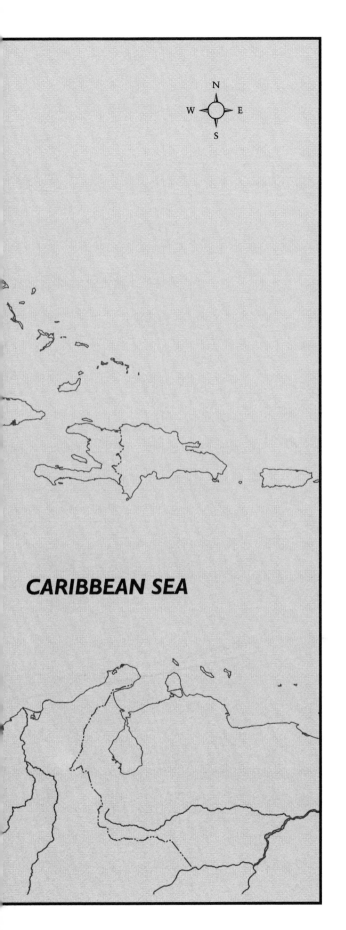

CARIBBEAN SEA

CHAPTER I

Karl Sapper, Walter Lehmann, and Franz Termer and the Study of Central America

Marilyn Beaudry-Corbett
and Richard M. Leventhal

Karl Sapper, Walter Lehmann, and Franz Termer and the Study of Central America

In the early part of the twentieth century, European scholars were preeminent in the social and natural science study of Central America. Their research areas included ethnology, archaeology, geography, linguistics, and epigraphy. These scholars left writings that are a crucial historical resource for contemporary scholars. Their detailed observations of traditional cultures and archaeological remains provide important primary data. Because their writings have been available only in the original German-language journals, the work of these scholars is unfamiliar to many researchers. This volume presents essays by Karl Sapper, Walter Lehmann, and Franz Termer, as translated by Theodore E. Gutman. Each essay is prefaced by a brief commentary on its continuing value for researchers.

CENTRAL AMERICA AT THE TURN OF THE NINETEENTH CENTURY

Throughout the mid to late nineteenth century, United States and European interest in Mexico and Central America increased as awareness of its geographic importance, and market potential grew. The Central American states, newly independent from Spain, held a rich supply of raw materials and commodities for overseas consumption. A new market for European and American manufactured goods, Central America was also a locale in need of construction and building projects. It offered investment opportunities for merchants, bankers, and engineers; employment opportunities for small urban proprietors and entrepreneurs; and agricultural opportunities for farmers and rural laborers.

Ephraim G. Squier, a former chargé d'affaires of the United States to the Republics of Central America, published a survey of Central American states in which he summarized their "geography, topography, climate, population, resources, productions, commerce, political organization, aborigines, etc., etc." (1858: title page). In a section on the market potential of Costa Rica, Squier shows coffee exports for 1852 at $609,984. In a section on a proposed construction of an interoceanic railway through Honduras, Squier includes information on sources for labor and material along with a prediction for revenue potential based upon the records of the Panama Railway. As is clear from Squier's report, parts of Central America represented an area to be closely watched by US and European economic enterprises.

When reviewing circumstances in Guatemala, however, Squier laments that "a system of exclusion against foreigners is rigorously pursued . . . [and] without colonization on an extended scale, supported by judicious laws, the useful arts can never be introduced or agriculture advanced, and the spasmodic attempt to encourage them, on the part of a few enlightened and patriotic citizens in the capital, can only prove melancholy failures" (1858:518). At this time the main staple product of Guatemala was cochineal (a dye). Coffee had not yet assumed major importance for reasons Squier illuminates:

> Some eighteen or twenty years ago, considerable plantations of coffee were made in different parts of the state . . . unfortunately, its cultivation was abandoned, owing to the insurrection of the Indians, in 1838 and 1848 . . . some attempts have been made again to introduce its cultivation . . . but hitherto not to any extent worthy of notice. (1858:525)

By 1863, just a few years later, a different situation existed. Cochineal exports were on the downturn because of the invention of a synthetic dye. The Guatemalan government was also actively encouraging the diversification of exports—including coffee, sugar, cotton, and other tropical products. These programs encouraged the expansion of capitalism and integrated Guatemala more closely into world markets. As Burns states:

> rapidly expanding coffee exports in the 1870s. . . exerted a formidable influence on the national economy: emphasis fell ever more heavily on commercial agriculture, the export2 sector, and international trade. . . . Lucrative coffee profits lured foreign capital and foreigners, particularly Germans, to the Guatemalan highlands. (Burns 1980:16,18)

William T. Brigham (1887) traveled in Guatemala, evaluating commercial circumstances and appraising the transportation systems. He saw that significant opportunity would result from a railroad and road system within Guatemala that could connect with others being planned in Belize (then British Honduras), Honduras, and southern Mexico. He states that "perhaps a hundred and twenty-five or thirty miles, in all, of single track, would result in quadrupling the coffee export of Guatemala" (1887:168). He laments that Guatemalan imports from the United States are smaller than those from Germany or France. By this time, the largest mercantile houses are German owned and coffee is second to sugar in importance of production.

In "A Winter in Central America and Mexico," Helen Sanborn writes of her travels throughout the region in 1886, with her father, James S. Sanborn of the Chase and Sanborn coffee company in Boston. Enjoying the company of German colonists in the Cobán area of Guatemala, Sanborn writes, "some of the Germans are owners of coffee plantations, others are merchants supplying the interior towns, and it is astonishing how many stores there are throughout the country, and what a vast amount of goods is imported, almost nothing being manufactured" (1886:75). Arriving in Guatemala City after an arduous overland journey, they lodged at the Gran Hotel:

> The proprietors were Germans, and most excellent gentlemen. . . . The Germans seem to be wonderful linguists, nearly every one we met could speak, besides his own language, English, French, Spanish, and Italian, all of which are quite essential to one doing business here, it is such a cosmopolitan city. (1886:111)

The Sanborns were granted an interview with President Barrios because "coffee, the principal export of the country, was the one subject in which he was most interested, and when he heard that a representative of a large coffee house in the United States was in Guatemala he sent an invitation for us to call" (1886:146). Sanborn described the coffee estates whose "owners are generally wealthy men, either Spaniards or Germans . . ." (1886:162) as well as the methods of picking and processing the beans.

In around 1913, B. B. Keable, an English writer, published a volume in Pitman's Common Commodities of Commerce series entitled "Coffee from Grower to Consumer." Stating that Guatemala is the most important coffee-growing country in Central America, Keable characterizes the product as being of excellent quality, thereby commanding some of the highest prices each year. Half of the country's export, according to Keable, went to Germany. In Costa Rica where coffee was still the most important crop, more than half went to the United Kingdom with only a small quantity imported by Germany. In Keable's judgment, Costa Rican coffee is "not the favorite kind on the continent of Europe" (N.D.:42).

MARILYN BEAUDRY-CORBETT AND RICHARD M. LEVENTHAL

As Central America became more closely linked with Europe and the United States through economic and commercial ties, it also became a focus for researchers. Americanist studies, which encompassed a variety of social and material sciences, had been established for some years on the Continent. This interest led to the formation of the International Congress of Americanists, which was organized by the American Society of France in 1875 in Nancy, France, with the stated object of

> contributing to the progress of ethnographic, linguistic, and historic studies relative to the two Americas especially for the time prior to Christopher Columbus and to put in touch people interested in these studies. (Congress International de Américanistes, Compte-Dendu de la Premiére Session 1875; translation by authors)

Representatives at these early Congresses ranged from high-ranking political figures (the Grand Duchess of Saxe-Weimar-Eisenach; S. M. Oscar II, King of Sweden and Norway of Goths and "des Wendes"; the Emperor of Brazil) to foreign service bureaucrats (the Nicaraguan consul-general in Brussels; the Brazilian consul-general in Liverpool; the Salvador minister to Paris), as well as others with academic and scholarly credentials (a member of the Brazilian Institute of History and Geography; the archivist of the Italian Navy; the conservator of the map section of the British Museum; the director of the Smithsonian Institution).

Early in the history of the Congress, which continues today, postcontact issues were avoided because of political concerns. Parallel Congresses were proposed where postcontact topics would be aired at sessions in the New World and precontact topics at sessions in the Old World. The advisability of holding a meeting somewhere other than Europe was hotly debated, but the question whether to schedule a Congress in the Americas went unresolved. A *session extraordinaire* was held in Mexico in 1895. Five years later at the next Congress, held in Paris in conjunction with

TABLE 1.1			
Topical organization of ICA sessions			
	1877	1900	1976
Anthropology and ethnology	x	x	
Ethnology			x
History of America and its discovery	x		
Linguistics and paleogeography	x	x	
Linguistics			x
Archaeology	x	x	x
History and geography		x	
History and ethnohistory			x
Human geography			x
Physical anthropology			x

the World's Fair, new bylaws were adopted and opposition to a New World venue was overcome. The 13th Congress took place in New York City in 1902.

Papers presented at the Congresses are divided into topically organized sections. The changing composition of the ICA sections during its first century is shown in table 1.1. The anthropology and ethnology section present at the 1877 and 1900 Congresses had changed to ethnology alone by 1976. Similarly in 1976 linguistics had been separated from the earlier linguistics and paleogeographic section. These changes reflect the gradual reshaping of the structure of anthropology's subfields and separation of associated disciplines.

The reassessment of anthropology as a discipline was evident in the US academic world as well as in conference organization. In the late nineteenth century in the United States and other parts of the world, anthropological theory had been based loosely upon an evolutionary model developed by Herbert Spencer and Lewis Henry Morgan. Unfortunately, the utilization of these evolutionary models was at best simplistic and at worst racist.

At Columbia University from 1896 until 1941, Franz Boas argued for the elimination of loosely argued evolutionary models and attempted to create a coherent discipline for the study of anthropology. Proposing a basic research initiative, which has since been termed "historical particularism," Boas promoted the collection of primary data and argued that only then could the process of inter-

TABLE 1.2
ICA sections in which papers were presented

	Sapper 1904–1935	Lehmann 1902–1912	Termer 1924–1949
Ethnology	x	x	x
Archaeology	x	x	x
Linguistics	x	x	x
History	x		
International relations	x		
Physical anthropology	x		
Geography			x

pretation begin. The quality of scholarship was, for Boas, directly attributable to the quality of the data recovered. He believed that reconstruction of culture history required a rigorous collection of all types of data—archaeological, linguistic, and ethnographic. Boas' approach to the study of anthropology still structures fieldwork and data collection today.

Because of Boas' own work and that of others who held similar views on the primary importance of accurate data collection, there exists a data set for the study of modern and ancient people throughout the world. Boas' inductive approach is exemplified by the writings of Karl Sapper, Walter Lehmann, and Franz Termer.

KARL SAPPER, WALTER LEHMANN, AND FRANZ TERMER

Karl Sapper (1866–1945) received a doctoral degree in geography from the University of Munich in 1888. He then traveled to Central America where his brother Richard was the owner of large coffee *fincas* (plantations) in Guatemala. Thus began his geological, geographic, and ethnographic investigations. He worked as a geologist for the Mexican government before returning to Europe in 1900 where he served as a professor at the Universities of Leipzig, Tübingen, Strassburg, and Würzburg. During his active retirement in Garmisch-Partenkirchen, he published articles on such topics as economic geography, the adaptation of human populations to different climates, ethnology, historical geography, and vulcanology. The scope of Sapper's contribu-

tions is evident from a simple list of the ICA sections in which he presented papers between 1904 and 1935 (table 1.2).

Walter Lehmann (1878–1939) was a student of Eduard Seler, a scholar who specialized in Maya art and Mexican picture writing but also studied pre-Hispanic astronomy, mythology, and calendrics (Seler 1990–1996). Lehmann followed Seler's path, translating Nahuatl texts and writing in the fields of ethnology, archaeology, and linguistics (see table 1.2). His professional career was spent as a professor at the Universities of Munich and Berlin.

Franz Termer (1894–1968), a student of Karl Sapper's, was appointed Professor at the University of Würzburg when Sapper retired in 1929. In 1939, Termer moved to Hamburg as Director of the Museum fur Völkerkunde with a chair at the University of Hamburg. His contributions in ethnology, geography, archaeology, and linguistics included presentations in these fields at ICA meetings between 1924 and 1949 (table 1.2).

ORGANIZATION OF THIS VOLUME

The first translated essay in this volume focuses upon Bartolomé de las Casas, an individual who has been identified as one of the few European advocates for Native Americans during the period of Spanish colonization. The recent quincentenary of contact between the Old and New Worlds has brought las Casas to the forefront of thought and analysis. The ongoing debate about the 500th anniversary focuses upon the sixteenth century as a period of discovery and developments as well as a period of destruction and cruelty. Villains are readily identified in the ranks of the Old World forces, and heroes are easily selected from the New World societies. Las Casas is, however, an enigmatic figure, for he bridges these two worlds. He arrived in the New World as a farmer in 1502 at the age of eighteen. Because of his perception of the cruelty toward the Indians in the New World, he took vows as a Dominican priest in 1522, at the age of 38. Examining the life of such an individual as las Casas—who is not clearly a villain nor purely a hero—shows that this debate is not unique to our time. It is clearly evident in Sapper's work from the end of the nineteenth century.

The second explores family organization and food, issues that are important in the study of modern and ancient human societies and about which Sapper collected essential primary data.

Q'eqchi' religion is the basis for Sapper's work in the third essay presented here. Much of this piece attempts to differentiate between religions—the native religion and Christianity. Richard Wilk's commentary and his recent work (Wilk 1997) demonstrate the impossibility of this task since the Q'eqchi' religious system is an entity unto itself. Sapper's work, however, allows us to gain an important glimpse of this religious system and its organization about one hundred years ago.

Sapper's report of his trip to the Pech (Paya) area of Honduras includes information about the native group's attempt to retain their ethnic identity including their language. Both commentators in that chapter describe the cultural resurgence currently taking place in the Pech territory. Additional examples can be found in other parts of Central America.

For example, over the past half century, some of the Q'eqchi' from Guatemala have moved into the southern part of Belize, into the Toledo District. They, along with the Mopan Maya, make up a large majority of the population of this district. These two Maya groups, the Q'eqchi' and the Mopan, are two of the most active indigenous groups within Central America fighting for their human rights in terms of land claims, environmental control, and political representation. Most recently these groups—represented by the Toledo Maya Cultural Council and the Q'eqchi' Council— produced, in association with the Indian Law Resource Center, the *Maya Atlas* (1997), the first indigenous compilation of land tied to the indigenous geography of a region.

The objective of Sapper's trip in 1899 to Costa Rica (chapters 6 to 8) from Guatemala, where he had been living since 1888, was to amplify the information gathered about the Guatusos by Bishop Thiel in 1896 and to add to the ethnographic map compiled by Henri Pittier a few years earlier.

Pittier, a Swiss civil engineer and professor of physical geography at the University of Lausanne, had accepted a position as professor at the Liceo of Costa Rica in 1887. He helped found the Instituto Fisico-Geografico de Costa Rica and wrote widely in the fields of natural history, geography, geology, and anthropology.

The inclusiveness of the interests of scholars like Pittier and Sapper is reflected in the scope of the reports in the last two chapters, written by Lehmann and Termer. Gathering linguistic information was the main objective of Lehmann's trip but he also communicated his very thorough observations about archaeological monuments and sites in Mexico and Guatemala. His allusion to Finca Chocolá as part of the Schlubach-Sapper holdings attests to the continuing importance of the German population in Guatemala. This company, which resulted from the consolidation of properties owned by different German families, was created after World War I and was first directed by David Sapper, the cousin of Richard and Karl Sapper. David had arrived in Guatemala in 1891 to help Richard manage the plantations. David became very interested in the language, customs, and traditions of the indigenous workers. Regina Wagner in her book *Los Alemanes en Guatemala 1828–1944* (1996:186) says he quickly understood Q'eqchi' thought and feeling better than other Europeans who had lived for years in the region. Included in Sapper's report on Q'eqchi' religious beliefs (chapter 4) is a prayer translated from the native language by his cousin.

The sociocultural role of Germans in Guatemala is reflected in the existence during Termer's and Lehmann's times of German-language clubs, cinemas, and libraries in Guatemala City. Wagner mentions (1996:342) great personalities of the academic world who gave conferences for the German community, including one organized by Termer in 1939.

By revisiting Central America with these early scholars, we can familiarize ourselves with the data sets they have provided and use them in forming our own hypotheses as well as evaluating our own interpretations of past lifestyles.

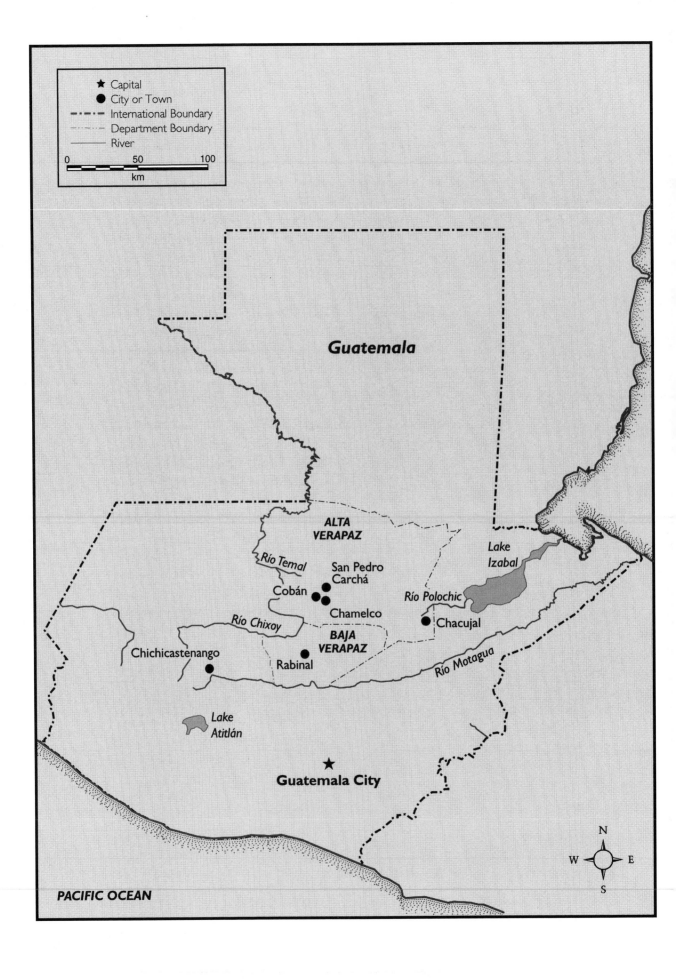

CHAPTER 2

Fray Bartolomé de las Casas and the Verapaz (Northwest Guatemala)

Karl Sapper

Originally published as
"Fray Bartolomé de las Casas und die Verapaz (Nordost-Guatemala)"
Baessler-Archiv 19(1936):102–107
Berlin: Verlag von Dietrich Reimer

COMMENTARY

Karl Sapper was a lifelong admirer of Fray Bartolomé de las Casas and considered him to be a hero of New World history. Sapper loved the Alta Verapaz of Guatemala above all and attributed the survival of its unique cultural components, the Q'eqchi' language and traditional customs, to the benevolent interference by las Casas in the course of Spanish conquest.

Sapper was one of the most perceptive and productive of the German geographers who began exploring all parts of the world in the final quarter of the nineteenth century. His quest for information knew no bounds in its wide-ranging approach to the study of Central American people and places. Sapper called his research "geography" but often did what we would identify as cultural anthropology, linguistics, or archaeology. He also incorporated culture history, ethnography, and prehistory into his geographical research long before such subjects became formalized as separate disciplines.

Many of the out-of-the-way places in Central America that he visited more than a hundred years ago are only now beginning to be revisited by anthropologists and archaeologists. By the 1890s Sapper was recognized as a world authority on the natural and cultural geography of Central America and was in great demand as a writer and lecturer in academic circles in his adoptive country as well as in Germany. Extremely influential in European academic circles but less so in New World ones, Karl Sapper had admirers in some universities in North America. At the University of California, Berkeley, the great geographer Carl Sauer, as well as his friends and colleagues Alfred Louis Kroeber in Anthropology and Woodrow Borah in Latin American History, accorded Sapper the status of a founding father of such fields as modern cultural geography, culture history, and historical geography.

Ted Gutman was a contemporary of Sapper's in the German academic world. While obtaining his Doctor of Law degree at the State University of Jena in 1932, Ted witnessed the officially sanctioned destruction of rational objective thought and the racist perversion of German academic disciplines, including cultural geography and anthropology, that was the result of Hitler's rise to power.

Both of us knew, admired, and worked closely with Ted Gutman for twenty years at UCLA and in the field. After being introduced to the writings of Sapper in the late 1970s, Ted quickly became an enthusiastic disciple, reading and translating many of his works. We had many long discussions about what Sapper's life, both as a field researcher in Central America and later as an academic in Germany, had been like. We mused about how disappointed Sapper must have been toward the end of his long career to see his rational view of faraway people and places sacrificed to political expediency and pseudoscience.

We also had a number of discussions with Ted about the lasting legacy of Sapper's great hero, Bartolomé de las Casas. Thus it is fitting that this volume of Ted's translations opens with Sapper's last homage to the Dominican humanist.

−Brian D. Dillon
Matthew A. Boxt

Fray Bartolomé de las Casas and the Verapaz (Northwest Guatemala)

When I arrived in the Alta Verapaz in Guatemala in 1888, where I then lived for twelve years, I was astonished by the extraordinary majority of Indians who, outside the cities and larger villages, appeared to be the exclusive population over broad stretches of the land. A population census held in 1893 confirmed that Indians in this department made up 95 percent of all inhabitants. This turned out to be a far larger percentage than in any other department of the country. When I became more involved with the history of the department it became clear that in the final analysis these statistics go back to the activity of a single man, the courageous, hated by many but also loved by many, defender of the Indians, Fray Bartolomé de las Casas.

This great man had already in his younger years energetically proposed a peaceful conversion of the Indians and had defended them later on in the book *De unico vocationis modo* (1876). He had first arrived in Guatemala in 1531. At that time Pedro de Alvarado had already conquered the largest part of the region of the present Republic of Guatemala. Only Indians living in the area north of the Río Motagua and east of the K'iche' empire and of the Río Chixoy had preserved their independence following three failed attempts at military conquest. No further attempts were planned, and the still-free territory was given the name Tezulután, Land of War.

After las Casas had returned to Guatemala in 1535 the local conquistadors laughed at his ideas and suggested that he try his luck in Tezulután. Without second thoughts las Casas asked for the permission of Bishop Marroquín, and Governor Maldonado decreed on 2 May 1537 that the local Indians could not be parceled out to anyone and that, except for the priests and the Governor, no Spaniard would be allowed to enter the territory within the next five years.

The already middle-aged man went to work with youthful zeal and wisely started his task by producing with two associates an educational poem in the K'iche' language about the fall of man and the life of Christ. The entire poem was set to music with accompaniment. Las Casas and his associates then taught this poem in its musical form to four Indian merchants who had traded for a long time in the Tezulután area. They memorized it and then went trading. In addition to their normal merchandise they took scissors, knives, mirrors, bells, and other Spanish objects to attract the attention of the Indians. They started their work in the principality of Rabinal where the prince, aware of unusual happenings, became interested in the religion. He established a connection with the priests, invited them to his capital, and was baptized soon thereafter along with many of the Indians. Not long afterward las Casas and his fellow priests expanded their activities and took Christianity to Cobán and its neighborhood.

It was very important for these enterprises that Pope Paul III issued an Apostolic Brief (Sublimis

Deus) on 10 June 1537 in which the Indians were expressly recognized as true humans and capable of converting to Christianity. This Brief, according to Remesal (1932, 1:177), is due to the influence of the Dominicans—Fray Bartolomé de las Casas, Fray Domingo de Betanzos, and Fray Bernardino de Minaya—since the last personally spoke with the Pope about it. Las Casas enjoyed great prestige at the court, and if he were one of the authors of this Brief, one may assume that he had his hand in the formulation of other important colonial laws of Spain.

Among the most important decisions achieved by las Casas for the Indians of the Verapaz was the prohibition of Emperor Charles V (1540), which stated that no Spaniard could enter the Dominican mission territory of Tezulután for five years (Remesal 1932, 1:226). As a result of this prohibition, which appears to have been extended repeatedly, the territory was for a long time spared the conflicts and encroachments that were customarily caused by Spanish immigrants in other areas. An even more important consequence was that the mixing of blood was prevented, which otherwise took place all over the Spanish American colonial empire.

This exclusion lasted until the end of the Spanish dominion in 1821 and caused the province, because of the progressive, peaceful conversion to Christianity, to change its name to Verapaz (True Peace) on 11 October 1547 (Remesal 1932, 2:191). The effect was that at least in the province's northern part, Alta Verapaz, which at first was economically less enticing, the Indians have remained up to now for the most part strong and pure. This was especially true in the country, away from the villages, despite a significant immigration of white and mixed elements since the middle of the nineteenth century.

When in the 1540s a Spanish settlement, Nueva Sevilla, was founded on the lower Río Polochic by settlers from Yucatán and Cozumel, the objections of the Dominicans in 1548 caused it officially to become extinct. This was something that Fuentes y Guzmán later regretted very much, because he assumed that the city would have been very important for the commerce on that side of the river. His view, however, was certainly incorrect. Larger ships could never have come to the place and, because the area is so unhealthy and in danger from floods, it has not been settled to this day. The location of the settlement is indicated on a map of Fuentes y Guzmán (1932–33, 2:297).

It is also possible that las Casas proposed a Cédula of 28 January 1541 (Fuentes y Guzmán 1932–33, 3:332, 425) which would have been important for the preservation of the Indians in the entire Spanish colonial possessions if it had really been carried out. This decree stated "que los Indios de tierra caliente no vayan á tierra fria ni por el contrario (that the Indians of the lowlands shall not travel into the highlands nor the converse)." In this decree, a basic truth of tropical acclimatization was proclaimed, a truth that to this day has not been taken seriously by modern colonial powers even though early Spanish observers, such as Pascual de Andagoya (Navarrete 1825–37)[1] and Oviedo y Valdes (1855, 4:347), had recognized it.

Even though las Casas had achieved or at least had worked for some of the government regulations for the maintenance of the Indians, he was not lucky with other measures. The population of Tezulután was widely dispersed throughout the territory, just as the Indians frequently are to this day in the Alta Verapaz.[2] This fact made the catechization of the natives much more difficult, and for that reason the Spanish missionaries in all areas promoted collecting them into larger villages (*reducciones*). This measure was first undertaken in 1541 (Fuentes y Guzmán 1932–33, 3:337), and later again in 1595 (Remesal 1932, 2:243). Even las Casas was convinced of the utility, even the necessity, of such a collection of dispersed inhabitants. With the help of the Indian prince right after his first successes at Tezulután, las Casas instituted this program despite strong resistance by the people.

Following the Spanish pattern he tried to

collect them into villages and towns away from their individual residences. This measure made the religious and political administration much easier, but it did not please the Indians who were accustomed to their old ways. In their opinion, no mountain was so beautiful, no valley so lovely, no water so good as in their former home, and they suffered great homesickness. This made them less resistant to illnesses, so that their number declined significantly in the reducciones. Not surprisingly, the Indians returned to their old places as soon as they no longer were under the direct supervision of their spiritual superiors. Of course, this took place only where the priests had not burned their former homes to make return impossible.

When a return to the old quarters was impossible but sufficient free land was available,* the Indians located their *milpas* (cornfields) at a greater distance from their village and lived there in the old style during the major part of the growing season. They returned to the village only after the harvest or for important religious festivals. I could still observe remains of this ancient custom at the end of the nineteenth century in the village of San Pedro Carchá, Alta Verapaz, where many houses stood empty during the greater part of the year and were lived in only before great festivities or when authorities mandated removal of the weeds between pavement stones.

Anyone who has spent the night innumerable times in isolated Indian huts and who has enjoyed a complete peace in them and their immediate surroundings understands very well that the Indians did not want to surrender this ideal condition, however much the missionaries tried to explain to them the advantages of living together. They felt that the limitation on their personal freedom when living in a community was a decided disadvantage, especially when they lived in tiled adobe houses rather than in leaf huts.

One advantage of the reducción localities was that the new living area was always nearby and at the same altitude as the old one, so that there were no difficulties with physical acclimatization. The cultural and psychological acclimatization required after the move, however, turned out to be extremely difficult for the Indians. Although las Casas has earned extraordinary credit for his manner of missionizing and through the elimination of Spanish immigrants that ensured the continued existence of the Indian people and their customs, he and his successor missionaries caused many of the Indians great damage by forcing them into reducciones. Psychic depressions and a considerable decrease in population were the results. At the same time, the missionaries were completely convinced that they acted in the best interests of the Indians, but they wore their European spectacles and were unable to understand the Indian life-style. Whatever came close to the missionaries' home conditions they found good while the natives frequently found the same things disagreeable.

There is one item in the Cédula of 9 January 1540 (Fuentes y Guzmán 1932–33, 3:4–51) that, if it actually had been carried out, would have been disagreeable to the Indians: namely, that Christian instruction be required daily at a set time. There is no doubt that, in addition to or even above the Christian god, the old gods continued to live in the hearts of the Indians. If the missionaries believed that in the Alta Verapaz and other parts of the Spanish colonial empire they could make convinced Christians of the Indians through frequent church visits and instruction, they deluded themselves.

---

* Many disadvantages resulted from collecting the Indians in the reducciones in the olden days in lightly settled areas with much free land. In these cases each settlement or village had its own substantial amount of *ejidos* (communal land). In later times and in densely populated regions the disadvantages were greater. When settlements and villages were consolidated, the new community was awarded some community acreage, but according to Milla (1882, 2: 92) the award was considerably less than the total of collective lands owned by each previous village or settlement. Thus, the inhabitants of the new entity were more disadvantaged since their former ejidos were taken over by the government.

In many cases and places even to this day, the non-Christian gods are prayed to, and heathen conceptions persist alongside Christian ones. Some may have believed that the community administrations would one day become guardians of Christianity, but it has not happened.

Las Casas would never have dreamed that at the beginning of the twentieth century these communal administrations would actually turn out to be the guardians of the old non-Christian beliefs in his beloved Verapaz. This I found out by a fortuitous accident. My trusted friend Sebastián Botzoc, who in 1894 had already dictated to me non-Christian prayers of his people (Sapper 1897: 287), told me casually one day after a monkey hunt that they really should not shoot monkeys since they were their elder brothers. I was at once reminded of the creation myths of the K'iche' Indians in the *Popol Vuh* (Brasseur de Bourbourg 1861: 31). When I continued to question him, he told me that he knew very little about these things but that yearly in his home village of San Pedro Carchá, the old traditions were communicated to the new members of the community council and community service. He said that if I were instrumental in his becoming a member of the community service, he would afterward tell me everything. Unfortunately, I was at the point of returning to Europe for health reasons, and so I could not take advantage of the offer.

I don't know whether this teaching still takes place for the benefit of the members of the community council in San Pedro Carchá or whether someone would still be willing to communicate what they had heard. Unfortunately I doubt it, even though at present the Indians are less anxious to preserve the secrets of their ancient religious beliefs than formerly. Texts that Schultze Jena (1933) has been able to obtain from the K'iche' of Chichicastenango are clear proof of greater willingness to communicate this information.

Las Casas and his collaborators lived long enough to witness the middle part of the Alta Verapaz being Christianized. Beyond that, the successes were very modest, something that evi-

dently was connected with the ethnic conditions. Remesal (1932, 1:201, 212) has described in detail how the prince of Rabinal favored the conversion to Christianity as well as the reducciones, but he did not report extensively about conditions in the Poqomchi' and Q'eqchi' areas.

These regions included somewhat more securely established and larger state-like political forms than in the Rabinal area. It is quite probable, however, given the position of the *cacique* (chief, headman) of Chamelco, that las Casas used the same tactics as had proven successful in the K'iche' area, that is, to gain influence over the people by approaching them through their prince.

Similar somewhat larger, state-like conditions most likely also existed among the Pipils in the southeastern Baja Verapaz but not among the Ch'oles, who reached to the Gulf of Honduras, nor among the Lacandones where missionary activity achieved sparse results. Those Ch'oles, who lived in the lower Polochic Valley not far from Chacujal and in the neighborhood of Lake Izabal, were already converted to Christianity by the mid-sixteenth century.

Success among the Acaláes and Lacandones was limited and transient. Pushed away by the Q'eqchi', they moved into the northwest of the Alta Verapaz and up to the Río Temal (Sapper 1906). The martyr death in 1555 of Father Domingo de Vico and his helper ended all further attempts at conversion (Remesal 1932, 2:377).

The reports show that the characters of the Indian tribes who lived in the Verapaz were quite different and that the Lacandones were evidently much more energetic and wilder than their neighbors. In all probability the Lacandones of northwestern Verapaz and the adjoining parts of the Petén were a separate division of the Maya tribes, as were the Lacandones who lived on an island further west of Lake Dolores and in its neighborhood, according to a small conserved fragment of their language.* The major attack against the Lacandones in eastern Chiapas from the city of

---

*   I can no longer sustain the opinion which I reported at the XV International Congress of Americanists in 1906 in Quebec that these were Ch'oles.

Guatemala and the attack against the Acaláes in northwestern Alta Verapaz by the cacique of Chamelco during 1559 were successful, but no long-term success was achieved for Christianity. Up to the present, isolated groups of Maya and Ch'ol-Lacandones have persisted in the desert of eastern Chiapas,* while they may have died out completely in the area of Guatemala. The same fate has befallen the Ch'oles from eastern Verapaz to the ocean, while the Ch'ol villages of northern Chiapas are in existence to this day. The main cause of the dying out of the Ch'ol villages in northern Chiapas or at least the decrease of population of both tribes in Guatemala was, on the one hand, the system of reducciones, and, on the other, the flight of the independent splinters of the tribes into more and more distant and frequently very unhealthy jungle. Insofar as these regions are located within the Verapaz or in southern British Honduras, they often have been resettled within the last fifty years rather thinly by Q'eqchi' Indians of the Alta Verapaz, despite many human deaths resulting from the difficulties of acclimatization.

The tribal strength of these people has remained outstanding because of the very personal ideas of Fray Bartolomé de las Casas about the best manner of Christian mission work and about the maintenance of racial purity despite human losses as a result of reducciones. Their strength is such that the tribe has recently been able to send its excess population into the empty rain-forest regions to the north and east of its original location without recognizable damage to the tribal entity that remained behind. This is perfect proof of the vitality that these people, now far more than one hundred thousand souls, have been able to maintain.

Notes

1. Sapper consulted an 1880 edition of this work, citing "volume 3, page 416." Because we have not been able to locate that edition, we reference the original and a recent reprint.
2. Sapper cites "F. Termer, Iberoamerikanisches, Archiv VII.1." We have not been able to determine the date or title of Termer's article.

---

* In the hinterland of Salto de Agua and Palenque, Ch'ol-speaking western Lacandones still exist; therefore, a recently expressed opinion has to be rectified (Soustelle 1935).

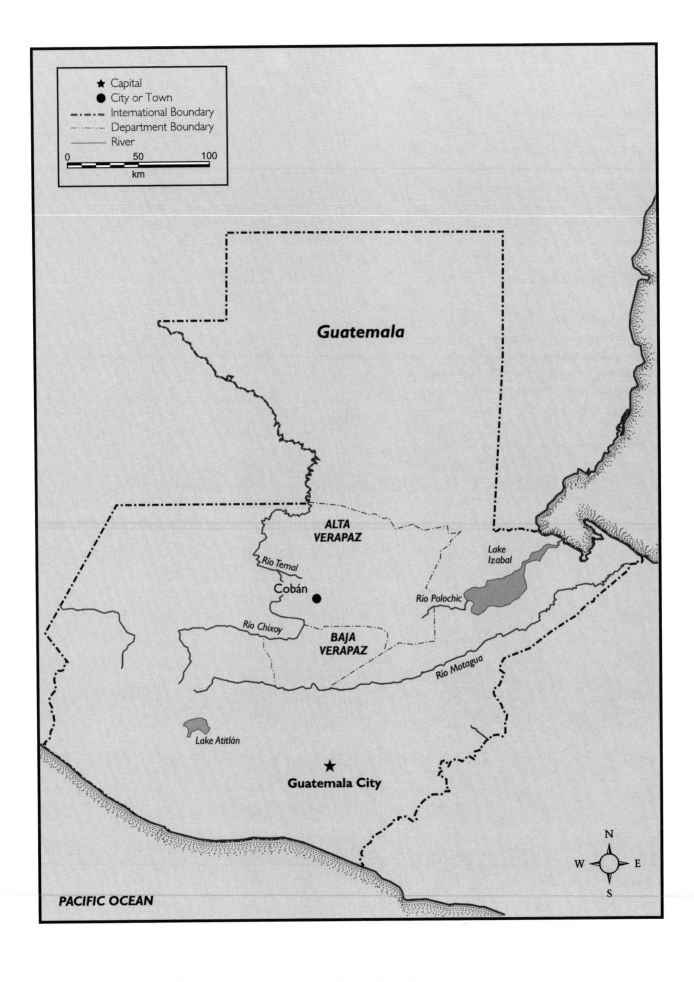

Capital
City or Town
International Boundary
Department Boundary
River

0   50   100
km

Guatemala

ALTA
VERAPAZ

Río Temal

Cobán

Lake
Izabal

Río Polochic

Río Chixoy

BAJA
VERAPAZ

Río Motagua

Lake Atitlán

Guatemala City

N
W   E
S

PACIFIC OCEAN

CHAPTER 3

Food and Drink of the Q'eqchi' Indians

Karl Sapper

Originally published as
"Speise und Trank der Kekchiindianer"
Globus 80(1901):259–263
Braunschweig: Druck und Verlag von Friedrich Vieweg und Sohn

COMMENTARY

Written and published after he returned to Germany from living in Guatemala, this article reflects Sapper's careful observation of all aspects of his informants' lives, even the details of housekeeping and food preparation. All of this was filtered through the eyes of a Victorian-era European. Thus, when reporting the response of Sebastián Botzoc to a question about the amount of time needed to cook a certain type of tamale, Sapper termed Botzoc's imprecise answer—"women know how long cooking takes"—as "naive." In all probability the Q'eqchi' informant was expressing the unimportance of such trivial details of women's tasks. A similar flavor of the period is seen from Sapper's allusion to "(James Fenimore) Cooper's warlike Indian figures, specifically their predilection for fire-water." While Cooper portrays both idealized and demonized Indian characters, other books emphasized alcohol consumption and other negative traits. Sapper had seen drunkenness among the Q'eqchi' but recognized that it occurred at specific intervals and contrasted with more customary demeanor.

Reading about the variety of foods prepared from corn reminded me of the centrality of this resource to the diet of indigenous Central American groups, as well as its versatility as a beverage, a gruel, and in tortillas and tamales. The fruits and vegetables Sapper recorded as being part of the Q'eqchi' diet are an interesting mixture of indigenous and introduced species.

I was struck by the continuity from the archaeological record to ethnographic times of aspects of the Q'eqchi' kitchen that Sapper recounts—the kitchen inventory, including pottery, gourds, and groundstone, as well as kitchen furnishings such as the corn crib, the raised platform on which bean pods are laid to dry, and a three-stone hearth. In our household excavations at Ceren, the village in western El Salvador buried by a volcanic eruption around AD 600, we have recovered a quite similar suite of pottery from a kitchen structure. Because of the unique destruction event, perishable materials such as wood, basketry fibers, and gourds have been preserved either as direct charred remains or burnt-out voids in the ash, from which casts using dental plaster have been made. In both a kitchen structure and a storeroom structure we have evidence of a raised platform built much like that seen by Sapper in the Q'eqchi' house. If I had been familiar with this account of the corn crib in the Q'eqchi' house when the Ceren project first started to expose a similar feature, I would have easily won the pool for identifying the use of this unusual contraption.

The similarity of the seventh-century archaeological households to those of the nineteenth-century Q'eqchi' cautioned me once again not to forget that events which change the larger society, such as the collapse of a powerful elite or invasion by a foreign power, may not be reflected in household patterns and that subsistence activities may persist in spite of social upheaval.

So, after reading Sapper's account of the food and drink of the Q'eqchi' Indians, close your eyes and visualize not only the inside of a traditional turn-of-the-century Q'eqchi' household but also early seventh-century El Salvador inhabitants processing their corn, drying their beans, and smoking their meat.

—Marilyn Beaudry-Corbett

Food and Drink of the Q'eqchi' Indians

Even though ethnological research appears to limit itself to investigations of the spiritual and material cultures of foreign people, their manner of subsistence, as well as the preparation of their food and beverages, deserve our attention. If in the following lines I discuss in detail the Middle American kitchen, I am afraid that the strict scientist will not appreciate the subject, believing it to be too mundane. On the other hand, I am hopeful of interesting German housewives, and I would feel extremely flattered were I able to achieve a certain amount of understanding among some of the German ladies for the gastronomical accomplishments of their brown sisters in the Indian huts of Guatemala.

Unfortunately I cannot invite the German housewives to try out the recipes given below, since the raw materials or tools necessary for their preparation are usually unavailable in Germany and also because normal Indian food does not initially appeal to the pampered European taste. I can, however, assure you from my own experience that in time one usually becomes quite appreciative of such food. After returning to Germany, I remembered it with pleasure and at times even with a sort of nostalgia.

Even though the Indian kitchen is essentially the same in all parts of Guatemala, I limit myself specifically to that of the Q'eqchi' Indians because I am best informed about the preparation of their food and beverages as a result of my years of residence in their midst. Their Indian names are given in parentheses.[1]

Corn (*ixim*)[2] is the basis of subsistence of the Q'eqchi' Indians, as it is for all tribes of northern Middle America. The important business of sowing and harvesting is accompanied by special prayers, ritual exercises, and rules of abstinence. As a result of their peculiar mixed attitudes, their ancient nature god Tzuultaq'a (Master of Mountain and Valley) is appealed to in this case rather than the Christian god. Since I have already written about these interesting customs, very little needs to be reported here to add to and correct my earlier paper (1895, 1897, 1904 [reprinted as chapter 4, this volume]).

In addition to the important prayers to Tzuultaq'a, some of the Indians do reverence to the Christian god in order not to insult him. In this case they go to church nine days before the sowing of the corn and burn some *copal* (incense from resin) and a number (12 to 23) of candles. During the five days preceding the sowing of the corn, one may not eat meat or herbs or *elote* (corn on the cob). The Indian must also practice abstinence not only during five days before but also for an additional sixteen days after sowing the corn. For this reason, recently married Indians do not generally participate in the sowing, leaving this job to older people.

The tall forest and scrub vegetation will have been cut down and burned beforehand; on the day of

Q'eqchi' Glossary

Word	Spelling in original	Spanish	English
ak'ach	ac'ach	chompipe, pavo	Turkey
akb', chochokl	akb, chochocl		Unidentified tree whose leaf is used to wrap tamales
aq'irk	aqúirc		Clean the milpa
awk	auc	sembrar	Sow
awleb'	aulep	morral (bien tejido)	Tightly woven shoulder pouch
b'oj	guatiboj	chicha	Corn beer
b'uch	buch	nixtamal	Corn prepared for making dough for tortillas and tamales
b'uchik	buchic		To prepare nixtamal
ch'ajok	chajoc	lavar	To wash (excluding clothes)
chakach	chacach	canasta	Small basket
chib'een li che'	chi ben li ché	tabanco, tapanco	Attic floor, raised bench or shelf
chiilan	chilan	pollo, gallo, gallina	Chicken
chiin	chin	naranja	Orange
ch'ima	chimá	güisquil, chayote	Pear-shaped fruit with large stone (Sechium edule)
chinamb'il	chinamvil	secado	Dried
chiqb'iltib'	chicvuil tip	carne cocida	Cooked meat
chiron	chiron	chicharrón	Crackling of skin and small pieces of roasted pork
ch'ixb'	chixp		Wooden rack to dry fruit or meat
chochokl see akb'			
ch'op	chop	piña	Pineapple
emel			Large cooking pot
hal			Ear of corn
hesok	hèsoc		Second grinding of masa
humal	humal		Green leaves of the corn
ichaj	ichaj		Edible herb (unidentified)
ik	ic	chile	Chile pepper, Capsicum annuum
is	is	camote	Camote; sweet potato (Ipomoea batate)
iswa	iscvuá		Tamale made from corn that is not quite ripe
ix	ix		Hulls of corn kernels
ixim	ixim	maiz	Corn
iximak	iximac	desgranar	To remove kernels from cob
joom	jom		Gourd, fruit of the calabash tree (Crescentia spp)

the sowing (25th of April or a few days after), the Indian goes to his field accompanied by a number of his friends. Each of the men brings along a fairly long pole with which he makes a hole in the soil; they then take the corn (ixim) out of a tightly woven shoulder bag (awleb') and throw three to five kernels into the hole, covering it lightly with soil afterward. Thus, they move in long rows slowly across the cleared piece of ground, which is often located on steep hillsides. They normally finish the business of sowing (awk) on the same day. After the corn has sprouted, the field is weeded (aq'irk) once or twice with a machete, and in October the harvest (q'olok) takes place. In the lowlands, sowing and harvesting take place some months earlier.

The healthy cobs are stacked (tusuk) in a special area; the smaller faulty cobs (xkok'al li hal, "the children of the corn cob") are stacked separately. The Indian stores his corn in his hut. The single room is his living room, bedroom, and kitchen. The fire is kept going night and day and is located somewhere on the floor of the hut. Cooking utensils are placed on three fairly large stones (k'ub'; tenamaste).

One can quickly name the total furnishing of the Indian kitchen. There is a large rounded cooking pot (uk'al), some other large cooking pots (emel), the small deep cooking vessels (xaar) that heat water, and a large, round, flat griddle (k'il, called comal in Spanish after the Nahuatl comalli).

To these are added certain water jars (tinaja; kukb' or kuch), which the Indian women normally carry on their heads when fetching water; ceramic cups (sek'), now mostly imported from Europe; cups made from the fruit of the calabash tree (joom); tall bottle gourds (su) and flat bottle gourds (seel) along with little baskets (chakach). Thus, the kitchen furnishings do not appear too scanty. Inasmuch as the house lacks a chimney and has no opening except the door, when the firewood is wet during the rainy season, the interior is occasionally filled with unbearable smoke. The smoke penetrates the skin and all garments, creating the characteristic odor noticeable in the Indian population.

In advance of preparing the numerous corn

dishes, the cover leaves (*humal*) are removed (*mich'ok*)[3] and the kernels are taken off the cob by hand (*iximak*). The corn is placed in a large pot (*uk'al*) together with cold water and some ashes or, more rarely, burnt lime. The mixture is stirred in (*yuli'*) and brought to a boil over the fire. After boiling for one or one and a half hours the corn is poured into another cooking pot; all of this takes place during the evening. The next morning the corn is washed (*ch'ajok*) in fresh water so the hulls (*ix*) of the kernels come loose, and the Indian woman begins to grind (*ke'ek*) the cooked mass of corn (*b'uch*) on her metate (*ka'*). Because the corn does not become smooth with the first grinding (*poch'ok*), it is ground a second (*hesok*) and a third time (*litz'ok*).

The corn dough (*q'em*) that results from this grinding forms the basis for all kinds of dishes, and their preparation takes up the larger part of the day's work of the Indian woman. In larger families, the teenage daughters have to help with grinding the corn; quite often one can also see little metates designed for use by little girls, to help prepare them for their future occupation. Similarly, 3- and 4-year-old girls accompany their mothers to the water source and carry some home in very small water jugs (*kukb'*) on their heads. From early youth they thoroughly master this skill, which is particularly difficult on account of the steep trails.

The most important corn dish is the tortilla (corn cake; *wa* or *xorb'il*), the mainstay of all Indian meals. The Indian woman takes a round piece of corn dough and forms it with her hands, twisting and patting (*xorok*, to form) the dough into a flat cake and putting it on the comal (*k'il*) that is placed over the fire. She turns it over after a few minutes, and then a few minutes later takes off this good tasting and very appetizing dish. The tortilla is wrapped in a napkin (*masb'a'e*) or put in a flat bottle gourd to keep it as warm as possible until mealtime.

I called this dish "appetizing" because the Q'eqchi' women are generally unusually clean and in the habit of washing their hands innumerable times during the day. Therefore these tortillas can be eaten with a better conscience than the bread of a European bakery, particularly since the trav-

Q'EQCHI' GLOSSARY

Word	Spelling in original	Spanish	English
ka'	ca	metate	Grinding stone
k'ab'inb'il is	cabimvil is		Camote cooked in sugar cane juice
k'ab'inb'il tz'in	cabimvil tz'im		Manioc cooked in sugar cane juice
k'aj	k'aj	pinol(e)	Corn flour prepared from roasted corn
k'aj ik	caj ic		Powdered dried chile
ke'ek	queec	moler	To grind
kenq'	quenk	frijoles negros	Beans (*Phaseolus vulgaris*)
k'il	qu'il	comal	Round flat griddle
k'orech	korech	totoposte	Tortilla prepared to last for several months
k'ub'	k'up	tenamaste	Three-stone hearth
kuch, kukb'	cuc, cucb	tinaja	Jar/jug for carrying water
k'uluj	c'uluj iscvua'		Tortilla with raw sugar added to the corn dough
k'um	c'um	ayote	Squash (*Cucurbita* spp)
k'ux, raxhal	c'ux, raxhal	elote tierno	Young ear of corn
kuy	cuy	cerdo	Hog
lamunix	lamunix	limon	Lemon
litz'ok	litzoc		Third grinding of masa
maak'uy	macuy		Unidentified wild plant
masb'a'e	masvael, masbael	servilleta	Napkin; cloth used for wrapping tortillas
matz'	matz		Warm beverage made from not quite ripe corn
mich'ok	michoc	pelar, quitar	To remove, peel
mox, moxl	moxl		Unidentified plant whose leaves are used for wrapping tamales
mux'aj	muipaj		Warm beverage made from tender corn
muy	muy	chicozapote, nispero	Fruit from the chicle or chewing gum tree (*Manilkara zapota*); Spanish is derived from the Nahuatl *tzico* meaning gum.
o	o	aguacate	Avocado (*Persea americana*); Spanish is derived from the Nahuatl *ahuacatl*
piyak'	piyac		Unidentified root of an edible tuber
pochb'i	pochvil	tamal(e)	Tamale
poch'ok	pochoc		First grinding of corn
pomb'il	pomvil	asado	Roasted
pomb'il is	pomvil is		Camote roasted over fire

Q'EQCHI' GLOSSARY

Word	Spelling in Original	Spanish	English
pomb'il tz'in	pomvil tz'in		Manioc roots roasted directly over fire
pox, t'zuumuy	pox, tzumuy	anona	Custard apple, mainly *Annona cherimolia* and *A. reticulata*
q'em	quem	masa	Corn dough
q'olok	koloc	la cosecha	The harvest of a milpa
raxhal *see* k'ux			
rax ixim	rax ixim		Literally "green corn," this is tortilla made from not-quite-ripe corn
raxtul	raxtul	ingerto	Injerto, a horticultural graft, *Pouteria viride*, a sapotaceous tree with fruit similar to mamey but smaller and smoother skinned
rax uq'un	rax uk'un	agua de masa	Literally "corn water," this is masa stirred by hand into warm water
saltul	saltul	zapote	Mamey (*Pouteria sapota*); Spanish is derived from Nahuatl *tzapotl*.
saqitul, tz'ultul	saquitul, tzultul		Larger banana
seel	sèl	tecomate (plano de forma esferica); jicara (para guardar tortillas)	Flat bottle gourd used to hold tortillas
sek'	sec	taza	Ceramic cup
sisamb'il wakax	sesamvil cvuacax	carne de res asado	Roasted beef
su	su	tecomates altos	Tall bottle gourds
sukuk	sucuc		Tortilla filled with cooked ground beans
t'akab'anb'il is	tacabanvil is		Simmered camote ready for consumption
t'akab'anb'il tzin	tacabanvil tz'in		Manioc cooked in water ready for consumption
taxanx	taxanx	tasajo	Dried beef
tuhanb'il *see* chinamb'il			
tul	tul	banano	Banana
tusuk	tusuc	ordenar	To arrange, stack
tz'eneb'ank	tzeneb	amontonar	Heaped up
tz'in	tz'in	yuca	Manioc, *Manihot utilissima* or *M. esculenta*
tz'ojl	tzojl		Unidentified wild plant
tz'ultul *see* saqitul	tzultul		
tz'uumuy *see* pox			
tz'u'uj	tz'uuj		Tortilla made from corn dough that includes cooked whole beans

eler most often can observe their preparation.

In spite of that, I must admit that I lived several years in Middle America before I found tortillas tasty. My palate took a long time to get accustomed to their somewhat strange taste. During the beginning of my sojourn, even though the cutest little Indian female would form and pound the corn cake in front of my eyes with her dainty hands, the product still appeared rough and disagreeable until hunger and time slowly taught me to appreciate it more.

Tortillas are normally prepared without salt by the Q'eqchi' Indians, but they do find it agreeable if they can add some salt. If they do not have salt available they usually add *chile* (*Capsicum annuum*) as this appears to help the digestion of tortillas. I came to this conclusion because my Indian porters used to neglect their chile during our travels as soon as they began eating the more digestible rice meals rather than their tortillas. They then would go back to eating chile whenever we entered areas where they could again get their customary tortillas.

Besides tortillas, corn dough (*q'em*) is frequently used to make tamales (*pochb' i*). The corn dough is heaped up (*tz'eneb'ank*) on the metate, then put into a little basket. Pieces of the dough paste are wrapped in the leaves of a plant the Indians call *mox* or *moxl* and again put in the basket. The following day this dough is placed in a lot of water and boiled for four or five hours until the tamales are fully cooked. Such tamales are always eaten in great quantities at the time of the sowing of the corn.

A variety of tamales called *ub'en* has cooked pork added to the corn paste, which is wrapped in leaves and cooked in the large pan over the fire for four or five hours. Sebastián Botzoc, my traveling companion and informant for many years, did not know the length of preparation, and so he added naively: "naq te'xnaw li ixq jo'q'e naraj li chaq'ak (well, women know how long it takes to cook the meat)."

Another variety of tamales is *xep*, prepared by mixing raw beans (*Phaseolus vulgaris*) into the corn dough; they are then wrapped in *akb'* or *chochokl* leaves and cooked in water for five hours.

In order to convey an idea of an Indian recipe I give one here in the Indian text with verbatim translation:

Toj rax   *li kenq'*   *te'xk'e*
Still green   the beans   one will put

chi sa' li q'em   *chiru li ka'*
in the corn paste   on top of the metate

lanb'il se' li akb',   *se ' li chochokl*
wrapped in *akb* leaves,   in *guajiniquil* leaves[4]

kiib'   *li xlanleb'*   *xpochb'al*
two   kinds of wrap   for tamales.

na'ok wi' chik   *se' li*   *uk'al;*
It is put again   in   the cooking vessel;

kela'   *chi sa'*
cold water   is put inside;

najt twanq se' li xam; hoob' honal tana.
long is it in the fire; five hours perhaps.

Another tortilla variety is the *sukuk*: milled or mashed cooked beans are put between two layers of corn dough and then roasted on the comal as tortillas would be. *Tz'u'uj* are tortillas that have whole cooked beans mixed into the corn dough and are also roasted on the comal.

An important variety of ordinary tortillas are the ones (*k'orech*) that can be preserved a long time: a form of maize cakes usually made in a large size and slowly dried out (*xujanb'il*) for about an hour over a low fire. These corn cakes, called *totoposte* by the Spanish-speaking population after the Nahuatl term,[5] easily last for one or two months. They are an excellent travel food for longer journeys, when fresh tortillas would get moldy in a very short time and ferment.

If the corn used for tortillas is not yet quite ripe, the Q'eqchi' Indians call the resulting food *rax ixim*, meaning literally "green corn." These tortillas taste better than those made from ripe corn, but they are less digestible. Tamales are also made from not-quite-ripe corn (*iswa*); these are normally wrapped in the green leaves of the corn (*humal*)

Q'EQCHI' GLOSSARY

Word	Spelling in original	Spanish	English
ub'en	uben		Tamale with pork or chicken
uk'al	uc'al, ucal		Large rounded cooking pot
uq'un	uk'un		Drink made by grinding corn three times, adding water, and leaving the mixture on the fire overnight; more specific than the general Spanish term, *atol(e)*
utz'aj	utzaj		Small stalks of sugar cane
wa, xorb'il	cvuá, xorvil	tortilla, torteado	Corn cake, shaped as a tortilla; Spanish is derived from a Nahuatl term
xaar	xar		Small deep cooking pot used to heat water
xep	xep		Tamale with raw beans (*Phaseolus vulgaris*) mixed into corn dough
xkab'e li utz'ajl	xcap li utzaj	panela	Raw sugar
xkok'al li hal	cocal li hal		Literally "children of the corn cob," these are smaller, faulty cobs
xorb'il *see* wa			
xorok	xoroc		To form
xpomb'al	pomval	asarlo	To roast it
xujanb'il	xujamvil	tostado, secado	Toasted, dried
xya'al	x tyaal		Beef broth
yatz'ok	tyatzoc		Squeeze out
yuli	tiuli		Stirred in

and taste delicious. If raw sugar (*xkab'e li utz'ajl*) is mixed into the corn dough from not-yet-ripe corn, formed into oblong cakes and roasted over the fire (*xpomb'al*), the result is called *k'uluj*,[6] a product that sometimes is offered for sale at the market in Cobán.

The corn dough (*masa*) is used not only for solid food but also for beverages. The refreshing beverage, *rax uq'un* (*agua de masa*; corn water), is offered to every traveler who visits an Indian hut. Masa is simply stirred by hand into warm water. This beverage constitutes a truly ideal, unusually digestible means of refreshment in that humid, warm, and extraordinarily mountainous land of Alta Verapaz. The European who is traveling on foot quickly gets to like it. While the Indians in the Alta Verapaz habitually mix only warm water with the corn dough for hygienic reasons, the Indians of southern Mexico and northern Guatemala prefer to drink a mixture of cold water and corn paste, which frequently is already fermenting (*posol*). The Q'eqchi' Indians do not care for that cold drink. They, however, like a warm beverage, similar to *rax uq'un*, made from not-quite-ripe corn which they call *matz*,' or another warm beverage made from tender corn (*mux'aj*). Indian women use the term *uq'un* (atole) to describe a drink made by grinding corn three times, adding water, and leaving the mixture on the fire overnight. The next morning the softened hulls are removed. The Spanish-speaking mixed population of Guatemala uses the word *atol* (after the Nahuatl term) to describe ordinary corn dough cooked in water.

As stated above, the long-lasting tortilla furnishes a part of the subsistence of the Q'eqchi' Indians during travel; another part of such travel food is made-to-last maize flour *k'aj* (called *pinol* in Spanish after its Nahuatl name). To prepare *k'aj*, uncooked corn is roasted on a comal, then milled on the metate; the resulting corn flour is mixed with warm to hot water to make a beverage that tastes unusually refreshing and agreeable. In contrast to the Verapaz Indians, the mixed population of Nicaragua mixes the corn flour into cold water, adding a small amount of cacao, sugar, and pepper, thus producing *tiste*, a drink that is so well known as the national beverage of Nicaragua that the inhabitants of Costa Rica refer to Nicaraguans as *pinoleros* (pinol drinkers).

To this day *rax uq'un* and the drink made from *k'aj* are the main beverages of the Q'eqchi' Indians, even though these drinks are increasingly being replaced by coffee. Maize is not only the main ingredient of these harmless and refreshing beverages but is also an ingredient in the alcoholic beverage of the Indians. *Chicha* (*b'oj*) was probably once made exclusively from corn. At the present time the Q'eqchi' Indians take very small stalks of sugarcane (*utz'aj*), mash them in a mortar, add an equal amount of corn flour from old, perhaps slightly spoiled corn and roll this in leaves. The leaves are put into a small ceramic pot that is hung about seven or eight feet above the fire and left for about three days. As soon as this mixture has become fermented, the Indians squeeze out (*yatz'ok*) large quantities of juice. They put this juice into a large pot to which they add a small amount of the fermented mixture. This liquid is then allowed to ferment for one or two days, to be consumed by them in incredible quantities during their feast days.

Since the production of alcoholic beverages is a state monopoly, chicha has to be produced secretly. For the various feast days the Indians buy some tinajas of chicha with official authorization. These are then displayed prominently at the locale of the fiesta for possible official inspection. They remain filled right up to the end, however, while the contents of countless hidden containers wet the always thirsty throats of the men, as well as their thirsty spouses and children.

If one sees on such holidays the drunken Indians, both males and females, one can observe that these people who are normally so gentle and quiet do have something in common with Cooper's war-like Indian figures, specifically their predilection for firewater. In defense of the Q'eqchi' people, these Indians are normally very sober, at least out in the remote rural areas where they are far away from the blessings of modern civilization, and they get drunk only during major holidays. This is not frowned upon, however, just as in pre-Spanish times even kings and the highest dignitaries got drunk right out in the open. Some were ordered to stay away from the feast in order to carry on the necessary business of the state during this period, while the king himself was incapable of conducting it (Milla 1879, 1:38).

The young ears of corn (*elote*; *k'ux* or *raxhal*) are also roasted and taste very good. Other than corn, beans (*frijoles*; *kenq'*) are the main food of the Indians. These are a black variety, *Phaseolus vulgaris*, that are sowed around the New Year and again at the end of June to be harvested after three months.

The newly harvested beans are stored for two or three weeks in the Indian huts on the floor of an attic (*tabanco, tapanco*; *chib'een li che'*) until dry.

This floor is constructed by laying branches from one roof support to an opposite one. When dry, the beans are taken down and the pods removed by beating them with sticks so that the clean beans can then be stored in bags.

The beans are placed in a large pot with cold water and some salt and cooked for three to four hours. The beans are then ready to eat or some lard is added to the drained beans before eating. For travel, the beans are ground on the metate, roasted with lard, and packed into green leaves.

The inseparable companion of all Indian meals is chile (*Capsicum annuum; ik*). It is not a nourishing food but is appreciated as an aid to digestion and during strenuous marches as a stimulant. Chile is sown in August and harvested after ten to twelve months. The fruit is dried on a wooden rack (*ch'ixb'*) over the fire and then is ready for consumption or conservation. For travel, the dried chile is ground on the metate and this chile powder (*k'aj ik*) is packed in maize leaves.

A frequent addition to an Indian meal is manioc (*Manihot utilissima; tz'in*).[7] Around the New Year a piece of the manioc plant is put into the ground and covered with some earth. The new plant sprouts within two to three weeks. The roots are harvested after about six months; their unwholesome bark is peeled off (*mich'ok*), and the roots are washed, cut up, and cooked for two hours in water without salt. The manioc is then ready for consumption (*t'akab'anb'il tz'in*). Now and then manioc is cooked in sugarcane juice (*kab'inb'il tz'in*) or the roots are roasted directly over the fire (*pomb'il tz'in*).

Just like the manioc, the *camote* (*Ipomoea batate; is*)[8] is simmered (*t'akab'anb'il is*), roasted (*pomb'il is*), or cooked in sugarcane juice (*k'ab'inb'il is*) and eaten. The root of an edible tuber (*piyak'*), grown only in the lowlands, is eaten only after roasting.

The *ayote* (*k'um*) is a pumpkin-type fruit; it is customarily sowed in August and ripens in April. It is cut into many pieces, placed in cold water, and then cooked without salt for three to four hours. It can also be steamed in sugarcane juice, which results in a delectable dish reminiscent of applesauce.

The *chayote* or *güisquil* (*ch'ima*) is the fleshy fruit of a liana-type plant (*Sechium edule*), which is normally cooked in water and tastes good. An edible herb (*ichaj*), as well as the sprouts of some other wild plants (*maak'uy* and *tz'ojl*), are also cooked quickly in salted water and eaten as vegetables.

Fairly well provided with vegetables, the Indian table's variety is further increased by a large number of fruits, the most important of which is the banana (*tul*). Of these, the small variety (*guineo*) or the larger (*saqitul* and *tz'ultul*) when ripe, are cooked in water, roasted over the fire, eaten raw, or sliced and baked in lard. The Q'eqchi' Indians eat the unripened bananas, either cooked or roasted, only in times of food shortages. The Indian tribes of Nicaragua and Costa Rica eat them regularly, since they contain starch and are an excellent food.

Other frequently eaten fruits include oranges (*chiin*), lemons (*lamunix; limones*), pineapple (*ch'op*), anona (*tz'uumuy* and *pox*), avocado (*o*), injerto (*raxtul*), zapote (*saltul*), chicozapote (*muy*), mangoes, and sugarcane.

Meat courses are relatively rare in the Indian kitchen since wild animals are hard to come by in the densely populated Alta Verapaz. Economic conditions do not permit the Indians the luxury of daily beef consumption. Meat is either cooked (*chiqb'iltib'*) or roasted (*pomb'il* or *sisamb'il wakax* [if beef]) on the spit. Beef broth (*xya'al*) often has condiments added such as salt, chile, onions, garlic, cabbage, or other plants. If the Indian is able to obtain a large amount of beef, he preserves it by cutting it into narrow strips, putting the strips into salt for a few hours, and then drying them in the sun or over the fire (*taxanx*; dried beef).

If the Indian is able to kill a hog (*kuy*), he first drains off the fat, then roasts the skin and small pieces of meat into cracklings (*chiron*). The meat itself is not cooked in water but rather dried (*chinamb'il, tuhanb'il*) on a wooden rack (*ch'ixb'*) over the fire, so that the lard drops into the flame and burns. Thus when the pork meat has become quite lean it is cooked in salt water and consumed. Most species of wild animals are treated in the same manner, since the Q'eqchi' Indians dislike fatty foods.

Chicken (*chiilan*) and turkeys (*ak'ach*) are

cooked in water, never fried. Eggs are eaten hard-boiled, though usually the egg is poached in water without the shell. Some progressive Indians have become accustomed to eggs fried sunny side up, but in general it is quite impossible to persuade the Indians to eat a soft-boiled egg. On advice of a doctor, I tried one day to give a raw egg to one of my porters as medicine against dysentery. The man told me in horror that he would rather die than eat a raw egg.

I have mentioned some of the beverages of the Indians that are made of corn and water. Besides chicha, hard liquor has found entry here as elsewhere, being the most obtrusive item of the European civilization. Coffee has also gained general distribution during the last few decades, since to a limited extent the Indians themselves have begun to grow it. Increasingly, coffee has even started to replace *cacao*, the ancient holiday beverage and luxury drink. Wild or cultivated, cacao trees grow only in the lowland climate belt. Since the Q'eqchi' Indians normally live in higher mountain regions, cacao had to be imported and became a rather costly beverage. For this reason its consumption is increasingly limited to special occasions.

The ripe cacao beans are taken out of their pods and subjected to a process of fermentation. After they are dried in the sun, and immediately before use, the beans are roasted on the comal and milled on the warmed metate. The cacao paste is mixed with sugar and warm water that is usually spiked with various condiments such as pepper, cinnamon, cloves, or vanilla. Because the cacao beans have been roasted and because a certain amount of fresh cocoa butter is mixed into the beverage, it has a fine aroma and an extremely agreeable taste, one that the European cook can never achieve with old cocoa powders lacking their oil. I particularly wanted to call attention to this fact in closing, because I am afraid that the rest of my story will not have engendered any special jealousy in the hearts of the German housewives over the cooking prowess of their Middle American colleagues.

Notes

1. In his original, Sapper used "Stoll's orthography" for native words. We have followed current linguistic standards.

2. Sapper used *hal*, which is the Q'eqchi' word for ear of corn. *Ixim* is the correct word for corn in this context.

3. Sapper used *mich'ok* or *b'uchik* as synonyms in the original but they are not. *Mich'ok* means to remove the corn leaves; *b'uchik* means to prepare *nixtamal*.

4. Neither *chochokl* nor *guajiniquil* has been identified.

5. Sapper called the language "Aztec."

6. Sapper used *c'uluj iscvua,'* which combines the word for tortilla (*k'uluj*) with that for tamale (*iswa*).

7. Sapper used *Manihot utilissima*; it is synonymous with *M. esculenta*.

8. Sapper used *Batata edulis*; it could not be located in any source. *Ipomoea batate* is the scientific name for *is* (*camote*, sweet potato) (Standley et al. 1970-73).

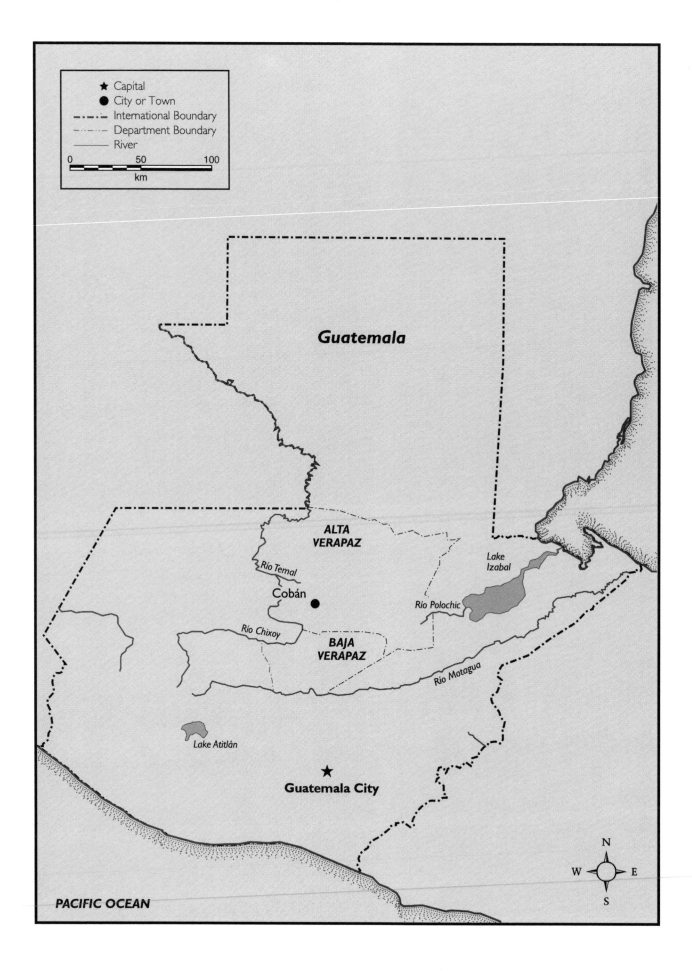

Guatemala

ALTA
VERAPAZ

Lake
Izabal

Río Temal

Cobán ●

Río Polochic

Río Chixoy

**BAJA
VERAPAZ**

Río Motagua

Lake Atitlán

★
Guatemala City

PACIFIC OCEAN

★ Capital
● City or Town
━·━·━ International Boundary
─·─·─ Department Boundary
─── River

0   50   100
km

N
W ✦ E
S

CHAPTER 4

Religious Customs and Beliefs of the Q'eqchi' Indians

Karl Sapper

Originally published as
"Religiöse Gebräuche und Anschauungen der Kekchi-Indianer"
Archiv für Religionswissenschaft 7(1904):453–470
Leipzig: Verlag von B. G. Teubner

COMMENTARY

The Tzuultaq'a still guide and watch over Q'eqchi' communities throughout Guatemala and Belize. People continue to burn incense to the Tzuultaq'a in their cornfields, pray to them in times of need, and make occasional pilgrimages to caves, mountains, and other holy sites where they can address them directly. In the Q'eqchi' village of Aguacate in Belize in 1980, I heard a sowing prayer almost identical to the one Sapper transcribes. Houses there are still splashed with pig's blood, though *ermita* burial houses are unknown.

Do these continuities suggest that the religion and culture of the Q'eqchi' are the same today as they were in Sapper's time? Is it a survival of ancient religious practices, as Sapper believed? Focusing on these continuities gives us only half of the picture. In other ways Q'eqchi' religion, and the rest of their culture, has been dramatically transformed by conquest, missionizing, and the imposition of a plantation economy. In this century it has been transformed by migration, a cruel regime of forced labor, political repression, and waves of Protestant evangelization and Catholic purification. After 500 years, does it still make sense to try to separate the "Indian" from the "Christian"?

In this chapter Sapper speaks with the typical tone of the "rational" Protestant about the strange magical customs of the Catholic Indians. He uses the "idols behind altars" theme, depicting Q'echi' religion as a superficial layer of imperfect or defective Christianity resting uneasily upon a deep stratum of unchanging pre-Hispanic paganism. This attitude is still common. Its subtle effect is to undercut the legitimacy and power of native religion, which is never seen as an integrated and coherent system worthwhile on its own terms; it always appears as a half-system. Sapper portrays the Q'eqchi' as really having two religions, one for the modern Christian city and one for the ancient pagan forest. Even the Christianity, however, is "contaminated by all sorts of superstitions," while the Mayan substratum has lost its ancient purity.

The "two cultures" thesis requires observers to distort time and history in peculiar ways that we now recognize as characteristic of much early ethnography. Sapper speaks as if the Spanish conquest actually happened recently and that the system he is observing reflects practices from the 1400s instead of the 1800s. It would seem from his account that the Q'eqchi' had been lost in time, unchanging until the moment Sapper appears on the scene. This time compression accounts for his remark that "already Christian elements are interwoven with ancient customs." If the Q'eqchi' were portrayed as people with a long, complex history, this would be quite unremarkable, since they had been Catholic for 350 years when he was writing.

The questions of continuity and change, of how conquest affects the cultures of both the dominator and the dominated, are as important in anthropology today as they were in Sapper's time. In this short piece Sapper opens a fascinating window onto an era when German colonial dominance of the Alta Verapaz was at its peak. Through it we can see something of the hidden transcripts of Q'eqchi' resistance and accommodation, as well as the intellectual superstructure upon which European power and hegemony were built.

–Richard Wilk

Religious Customs and Beliefs of the Q'eqchi' Indians

After the armies of Spain, accustomed to victory, had conquered most of Guatemala, they came upon such energetic resistance in the region of Tezulután that they made no further attempts at conquest. At that point the very religious Dominican monk Bartolomé de las Casas felt the time had come to put his ideas of peaceful conquest and Christianization into practice. He received permission on 2 May 1537 to launch his enterprise, which succeeded so brilliantly that ten years later don Felipe, representing Emperor Charles V of Spain, changed the name of Tezulután (Land of War) to Verapaz (True Peace). Later, in 1555, he even recognized the old laws of the local Indians.

This region honored its name because of its out-of-the-way location, lack of mineral resources, original exclusion of Spanish colonists, proper behavior of the Dominicans, and peaceful character of the Indian population. Since that time comparative peace and quiet have reigned in this Indian region. True and complete peace has never existed, because the new religion, despite its establishment alongside the old, has not been able to replace it entirely and frequently remained foreign to the feelings of the Indians. The Christian god is, after all, the god of the foreigners. He may be accorded a certain dominant position vis-à-vis the gods of the Indians in approximately the same measure to which they accept mixed bloods and whites compared to other Indians. They live far from the centers of European civilization and therefore have not been strongly influenced by new ideas. They are generally of the opinion that the Christian god is more concerned with the foreigners than with the Indians and that he therefore does not take a great interest in those things that mean the most to them.

Such an attitude is current among the Indians of the Alta Verapaz despite following Christian religious practice for hundreds of years, because thorough religious instruction by the sparsely available clergy was impossible with such a widely dispersed population, which even to this day is 95 percent Indian. The people of the more southerly Baja Verapaz are more exposed to the influence of ladinos.[1]

Currently, school attendance is obligatory, and even plantation owners are forced by the government to provide a place for a school and to hire a teacher. This practice has not changed things, however, because the Indians generally refuse to send their children to school and would rather move on than be forced to do so. In order to maintain at least a certain general measure of knowledge of the Christian faith, the earlier Catholic priests had translated the teachings of the faith into the Indian language and would not consecrate a marriage unless both partners had proved a certain knowledge of the catechism. This rule has been maintained until now, but it has been unable to produce a proper understanding of the Christian teachings among the Indians.

Q'eqchi' Glossary

Native word	Spelling in original	Spanish	English
b'oj	guatiboj	chicha	Corn beer
ch'ol winiq	Cholguink	lakantunes	Lacandones; inhabitants of northwest part of Alta Verapaz
ichb'olay	icvolai	barba amarilla	Fer-de-lance snake (*Bothrops asper*)
ikb'olay *see* ichb'olay			
li Qawa' Kurus	li cacvuá cruz	Nuestro Padre la cruz	Our Father the Cross (the Christian god)
li Qawa' Saq'e	li cacvuá sakké	Nuestro Padre el Sol	Our Father the Sun
li Qawa' Tzuultaq'a	li cacvua' tzultaccá	Nuestro Padre, el Señor de la Montaña y del Valle	Our Father, the Lord of Mountain and Valley
masb'a'e	masvael, masbael	servilleta	Napkin; cloth used for wrapping tortillas
tz'aamank	Chama		Housekeeping exam of the bride
Tzuultaq'a	Tzultaccá		Q'eqchi' god
wa'tasanb'il	guatasamvil	inaugurado	Inaugurated
winaq			Maya month of 20 days
xinlub'	xinlup		I am tired

It seems to be difficult for the Indians to see the various figures of God and his saints as just pictures. They not only call each of these paintings or sculptures a "god"—the same as a pagan idol using the Spanish word *dios*—but they believe that these pictures are actually alive.

Before the feast day of the patron saint of an *ermita* (hermitage; church), his image is carried in its ark or chest by a special commission to the church of the nearest village so that the saint can hear Mass once more. If this necessitates an overnight encampment, a cloth is placed over the ark and the following morning, before resumption of the march, the leader of the commission carefully lifts the cover to make sure that the saint is already awake.

On the day when the patron saint of Cobán, Santo Domingo, celebrates his name day, they not only carry him in a procession through the town but they also carry all other images of saints to him so that they can express their congratulations to him. The Indians consider not just images of saints but even single wooden crosses to be alive

under certain circumstances or at least at certain times. My porters, for instance, have assured me seriously that they have observed movement of some crosses along the path.

It is the pride of the Indians to have a large number of images of saints in their churches. On one occasion my Indian companions stumbled by accident into a Protestant church in Belize City. They told me afterward, full of pity, that the congregation must be poor people, because they had only one god in their church. They do not seem to understand the unity of God, despite the fact that they have learned the catechism by heart. Once I witnessed a discussion about whether Christ and the Nazarene were two gods or one; the dispute was finally resolved among the Indians present to the effect that two different personalities were involved.

It is therefore not surprising that they believe that my god, the god of the Protestants, is a different one from theirs. They also thought that in British Honduras they would no longer have to pray, because the god there would speak English and not understand prayers in their language.

Thus within their version of the Christian faith a number of gods exist, even if not by their open admission since the letter of the catechism denies it. Under such circumstances it becomes understandable that a few pagan gods could maintain their place in the Indians' hearts comparatively peacefully alongside the Christian god. I never saw images of these pagan god-figures nor ever heard even a hint of their existence.

Before the conversion to Christianity the Q'eqchi' Indians had numerous idols as proven by excavations. At present the Q'eqchi' inhabitants of the northern Alta Verapaz have two pagan gods: the sun and the "Lord of Mountain and Valley." Of these the first is the Lord Sun, a singular personality, who provides a multitude of services to the Indian and therefore is venerated most highly without a need for sacrifices. Sacrifices are unnecessary, because this benevolent god does all these services without them; he is also too far distant to hear prayers. Just the same the grateful Indian always thinks of all the good deeds that the sun provides for him. The sun gives light and warmth to the earth, dries out the humidity, and dries out the felled underbrush of the *milpas* (cornfields) so that they can be burned and planting becomes possible. The sun helps the corn to grow and ripen, thus guaranteeing the Indians' existence and therefore being called justifiably "our Father the Sun" (*li Qawa' Saq'e*) in contrast to *li Qawa' Kurus* (our Father the Cross, that is, the Christian god).

If the sun is for the Indian a distant god, his other main pagan god, *li Qawa' Tzuultaq'a* ("our Father, the Lord of Mountain and Valley") is a multiple personality who lives nearby. Almost every village and every settlement has its own Tzuultaq'a. Occasionally, one hears remarks that one Tzuultaq'a was considered stronger than another and that he protected his people better from sickness and other dangers.

Ordinarily the Indians turn to the Tzuultaq'a of their own neighborhood. On especially important occasions, such as the sowing of the cornfield, they implore not only the Tzuultaq'a of the home area but also those of neighboring settlements and even those of especially important distant points so that no difficulties may arise. In a prayer I recorded earlier (Sapper 1897:292, see sidebar), which is used three days before the sowing of the corn, besides the Tzuultaq'a of their own location, two other Tzuultaq'a of nearby settlements are implored as well as three apparently important similar gods from distant localities.

The Tzuultaq'a live in large caves in the mountains of the Alta Verapaz; some of them are male, some female. The male Tzuultaq'a live in poorly watered mountains, the female in mountains with many springs. Flooding is a sign of the fiestas that the Tzuultaq'a celebrates in his subterranean domain. There Tzuultaq'a reclines in a hammock suspended between two huge *ichb'olay*.[2] Snakes are the servants of Tzuultaq'a who punish the misdeeds of people through their bite; depending upon the severity of the misdeed, Tzuultaq'a sends more or less poisonous or nonpoisonous ones.

He can also punish human offenses by sickness or by a lightning strike; lightning strikes at the point to which Tzuultaq'a throws his stone axe. Water is sacred to him; for that reason, a hot object may not be cooled in running water. The

Prayer to Tzuultaq'a
Three Days Before Sowing the Corn

Translated into German by David Sapper

You, oh God, you my Master, you my mother, you my father, you Master of Mountains and Valleys!

Today is the day, now is sunlight! I give you a little of your food, a little of your beverage! And it is not much and not much good what I give you.

Now I have burned the sacrifice in the hour of the day, the hour of sunlight. I will do the same in three suns, in three days!

It does not hurt you, it is no trouble for you to show yourself to my soul, to my body. It does not hurt you, it gives you no trouble to show me my food and my beverage, you my mother, you my father, you angel, Master of Mountains and Valleys.

Who is my mother, who is my father? You, for sure: on account of the clearing of the cornfields, the tilling, because of the food, of the beverage!

Now, oh Master, I am at your feet, at your hands, so that my corn may sprout. You my mother, you my father, you Master of Mountains and Valleys! Let it sprout!

Now is the day, now is the sunlight! it will be the same in three suns, in three days. Let it sprout, you Master of Pekmo' (local Tzuultaq'a), you Master of Kojaj (neighboring Tzuultaq'a), you Mistress[3] of Chi'itzam (distant but powerful Tzuultaq'a), you Master of Xekab'yuk, you Master of Q'anwen, you Master of Chakmayik (animals and probably plants)!

In three suns, in three days (the corn seeds) will find their place before your mouth, in front of your face.

It does not hurt you, it is no trouble for you to protect him from all that may happen to him, because I plant it, because I cover him in front of your mouth, in front of your face.

May you hide and reinforce all of your (for him damaging) children (animals and probably plants).

Throw them across thirteen mountains, across thirteen valleys! I do not wish it to die and fade away, rather I wish that my corn germinate and sprout.

After seven suns, after seven days I will look after the sprouting, after the germination that breaks the earth and comes into the daylight; after that I will replant.

In the name of the Father, of the Son of God, and of the Holy Ghost!

animals of water, earth, and air belong to him; therefore, fishing and hunting are only allowed after prayers and sacrifices to Tzuultaq'a. Animals may not be killed by burning in an open fire.

Like the animals, plants belong to him also, especially the useful plants, and certain sacrifices must be offered to him before sowing or harvest. No edible part of a killed wild animal may be left and allowed to rot nor any useful plant wasted. Occasionally, when some corn seeds have been spilled and have sprouted in the moist soil, an Indian will dig them up, leaving some earth around their roots, and transplant them to his cornfield so they do not wilt. Those who do not do this will be punished later by bad luck in hunting or in their fields.

It is only natural to try in every way to get Tzuultaq'a into a favorable mood since agriculture is the foundation of the people's subsistence and the results of hunting and of fishing certainly make meals more agreeable. This is done by prayers, which are passed along by oral transmission in old-fashioned form, with the addition here and there of Christian elements, of course. This is also attempted by sacrifices of flowers or branches of trees, and by burning incense, as well as by mortifications (abstinence from sexual relations or from eating meat, certain vegetables, or other foods). All this corresponds precisely to pre-Christian customs, even though their observance is probably less strict.

The extent of the sacrifices or mortification is different depending upon the importance of the action for which Tzuultaq'a's favors are needed. For instance, the Indian needs to practice complete sexual abstinence five days before and sixteen days after the sowing of corn (a total of twenty-one days, or an old Indian month [*winaq*] plus one day). For the sowing of beans or chile (*Capsicum annuum*), only a few days of abstinence are sufficient and then only for those who plant larger quantities of these useful plants for commerce.

Already Christian elements are interwoven with the ancient customs. Thus nine days before the sowing of the corn, a pilgrimage is made to the church where some incense is burned and 12 to 23 candles are lit. Despite all preference for Tzuultaq'a, the Indian is surely aware of Tzuultaq'a's subordination to the Christian god. This subordination takes place only in the more populated areas. Uninhabited or sparsely inhabited forest regions are still exclusively under the domination of Tzuultaq'a—no wooden crosses have been erected at the height of passes or at crossroads. If an Indian intends to take up residence in such an uninhabited area, he will first walk around as much land as he can in one day and fell a little tree at each of the four cardinal points. He will return after one year, sacrifice to Tzuultaq'a by burning copal, and start his cornfield in the direction to which the smoke of the burning incense points.

Even after permanent settlement Tzuultaq'a remains the sole ruler—no prayers are made to the Christian god yet. Only after a larger number of families have settled alongside each other and an ermita has been established with its obligatory pictures of the saints are Christian services initiated. Tzuultaq'a now says *xinlub'* (I am tired), and up to a point he cedes his supremacy to the mightier Christian god.

The territorial boundary of the Christian god advances farther as a result of the rapid expansion of the Q'eqchi' Indians into the rain forests of the northern Alta Verapaz; the total domain of Tzuultaq'a shrinks more and more. Currently, it is still sufficiently extensive and even the pious Christian Q'eqchi', to the extent that he still adheres to his traditions, does not dare to pray there to the Christian god, because Tzuultaq'a would be insulted.

In a similar manner the Q'eqchi' respected the unknown god of the Lacandones as long as we traveled in his territory. They all seem to have a certain tolerance as they are by nature a peaceful people. The Indian who lives with his family deep in the rain forest and prays to Tzuultaq'a becomes a Christian again as soon as he returns to the region of the Christian god. Even at the border markers of this region, made of simple wooden crosses alongside the path, he takes his hat off as if he had never left the Christian district.

A submissive respect manifests itself in the

manner in which the Indian steps up to the picture of the Christian god and the saints when he prays to them. If he speaks of them one feels as if he were making submissive genuflections in front of them. How different when the Indian during the solemn quiet tropical night leaves his camp in the virgin forest and steps in the direction of the morning's march. On a large green leaf he puts the incense that he has carried along, burns it with glowing coals, and says his traditional prayers to Tzuultaq'a, the Master of Mountain and Valleys, the Master of Trees and Lianas (Sapper 1897:289, see side-bar). Then the Indian's confidence shows that his longtime god will help him, the god who knows all the Indian's wants and needs much better than any foreign, proud Christian god.

The solemn manner in which the Indian spoke to his god freely and with confidence impressed me even during normal safe wanderings. I will never forget the strong impression I got one time deep in the wild rain forests of British Honduras after long days of hunger, when at dusk the oldest of my Indian companions hailed Tzuultaq'a and begged for a successful hunt, even though he was unable to produce the normal sacrifice (Sapper 1902:38). Then during the same night for the first time in a long while we heard the ugly screaming of the howler monkeys, which at that point was music to my ears. I could not help the heretical thought that the good god had heard the confident prayer of the men, even if it was not directed at Tzuultaq'a's exact address.

The Q'eqchi' Indian meets the Christian god with the deepest respect; he also embraces with warmest thankfulness the Father Sun who is so beneficial and so far distant that not even the Christian god can diminish his stature. When it comes to Tzuultaq'a, the Indian is filled with a mixture of love and fear. Even though he fears him under certain circumstances, his heart nevertheless embraces Tzuultaq'a because he is, so to speak, the god of his own brown race. He can hardly imagine the Christian god with other than the white skin of the partly feared, partly hated European whose skin he, in his heart, despises a little.

With a certain sigh the Q'eqchi' fulfills his obligations towards the Christian god; even if the

Evening Prayer to Tzuultaq'a on the Road

Translated into German by David Sapper

You, oh God, you Master of Mountains and Valleys! I have given you a little of your food, of your beverage [meaning the sacrifices]. Now I pass under your feet, under your hands [under your power], I, a traveler.

It does not hurt you, it does not trouble you to give me all sorts of large animals, small animals, you, my Father!

You have a large number of animals, the wild turkey, the wild pheasant, the wild boar; show them to me, open my eyes, take them and put them into my path.

Then I see them, I observe them; I am under your feet, under your hands; I am in luck, you Master of Mountains and Valleys. In your power, in your name, in your being everything possible is available in abundance; I would like some of all of it. Today I may have to eat my corn cakes dry although I am in a rich hunting region; God may see that nothing living is here; perhaps I only bring a wild turkey, I drag him here.

Now I see, now I perceive, you my God, you my mother, you my father! It is only what I say, what I think; it is not much, nothing special of your food, of your beverage, that which I have dragged here. Whether it is so or other, what I say and what I think is: God! you are my mother, you are my father.

Now I am going to sleep under your feet, under your hands, you Master of Mountains and Valleys, Master of Trees and Master of Lianas.

Tomorrow we have another day, tomorrow we have the sunlight again!

I do not know anymore where I will then be.

Who is my mother, who is my father? Only you, my God.

You see me, you protect me on every path, in every darkness, at every impediment that you hide, that you may remove; you my God, you my Master, you the Master of Mountains and Valleys.

It is only this I say, what I think: be it more, be it that it should not be more; what I have said; you tolerate, you forget my misdeeds.

service is easy it has a disagreeable side since often it touches a very sore point with the Indian, his wallet. This is much less the case with Tzuultaq'a despite the fact that the incense largely needs to be imported from great distances (for example, from Motocintla in the Mexican state of Chiapas). On the other hand, the ritual for Tzuultaq'a requires certain bodily sacrifices, flagellations, and abstinences of various kinds. Quite a few Indians are willing to abstain from sexual relations for 40 days (two *winaq*) and to fulfill the three days of prayers with the entire family in order to be allowed to burn candles personally for Tzuultaq'a in his cave and possibly to see him face to face on this occasion in his hammock supported by ichb'olay ropes.

Even though his pagan religion is much closer to the heart of the Indian than modern Christianity, he cannot possibly separate Christian influence in all his beliefs. The old manners survive in all his memories; the form of the purchase of brides generally remains the same (Sapper 1897:279 ff). Locally they even still demand a sort of examination on housekeeping of the bride (*tz'aamank*); the bridegroom still acquires a new name from the object or happening that impressed him most after the wedding night. The old "Nagualism" is occasionally still detectable, and the Q'eqchi' believe to this day that the neighboring *ch'ol winiq*—that is, the pagan Lacandones—can transform into jaguars.[4]

The various old customs have lasted up to the present, but the foreigner finds out about them only by accident, even if he lives among the Indians for many years. Still the Christian influence is more or less clearly discernible and shows up recently even more strongly in cities bordering on the Maya areas. One can see that particularly well from the belief of the Indians regarding life after death.

The belief of a continuous life after death has since olden times been in the Q'eqchi' blood; they specifically believe that after death they have to repeat the trips they made during their life. For that reason one gives the dead a new suit of clothes and, if possible, puts a reed mat into his tomb so that the wandering soul has a place to sleep. Furthermore, the deceased gets a ceramic pot, a cup, a wooden drinking bowl, and a *masb'a'e* (a cloth or napkin into which food can be wrapped), also a hat, sandals, a tumpline and net, fire-making equipment, and a kind of head covering made of palm leaves, in short the complete travel equipment. The only item left out is the now customary but formerly unknown woolen blanket, which is believed to bite the soul in the grave.

The deceased is given a rosary in his right hand so that the Christian element is represented. It is important that the clothing be in good condition. If the Indian looks death in the face far from home, his most important task is to repair his clothing so that it will endure the strain of the long travels in the next world; the Indian is ashamed if he cannot appear in proper clothing in front of strangers.

In case something has been forgotten, the soul of the deceased will appear to the nearest relative in a dream and call attention to this omission. Since reopening the grave is not possible, they put the missing item into the grave of the next deceased person, requesting that it be delivered to the correct owner. No food is given to the deceased, because the soul does not have an earthly body and therefore does not require nourishment.[5] Tzuultaq'a furnishes souls in the other world with the necessary food. It could happen, although quite rarely, that people cannot again find all those formerly traveled paths; therefore wooden crosses are erected at the crossroads. At these locations the soul lifts its hat and asks for direction, whereupon the cross gives the necessary information. The soul does not need to retrace travels on the water or in areas with foreign languages because it goes only as far as it has strength to walk on its own.

Several times my porters speculated on how I would fare after death. Even though I made the trips on foot just as they did, I did not carry my own luggage and was therefore dependent upon the help of others. The question was usually resolved to the effect that in the other world they would again accompany me on my travels and carry my luggage.

The living Indian rests for a time at home after each trip to renew his strength before he undertakes a new journey, and so does the soul later on. For this reason it is necessary to establish a proper rest house for the returning and resting souls. Several Q'eqchi' families cooperate to build a cemetery house which at the same time serves as a place for sleeping, feasts, and assemblies, as well as for religious services. For that reason it is now generally called by the Spanish name ermita. If such a house has been constructed it is consecrated and inaugurated (wa'tasanb'il); all members of the cooperative assemble during the evening with their children and relatives at the ermita and drink chicha (b'oj). (See chapter 3, this volume.)

At midnight they kill a pig, and the posts and beams are splashed and smeared with its warm blood. Then the women cut up the pig and cook the meal for the festival, which starts as soon as the sun rises the following morning. In a similar but simpler manner the residences, as well as the boats of the Q'eqchi's, are consecrated.* The ermita is not only the burial house for the particular cooperative society but also the center of the social life within that small circle. A separate administrative group takes care of all necessary work, and its members advance into the upper echelons after first serving in the lower ranks. The treasury of the ermita gives loans at high rates of interest to the members of the group. On personal projects that can only be carried out properly by a larger number of people, such as sowing maize, harvesting, and possibly building a house, the participants in a cooperative help one another, but the beneficiary is expected to remunerate his helpers with a big meal.

The biggest cooperative job continues to be the upkeep of the ermita as a burial house. That is because it is necessary to make sure that no rain, moonlight, or sunshine touches the graves and bothers the departed souls when they have returned exhausted from their travel to their home base. Then they can comfortably talk to their associates before departing on a new trip.

When the ermita has become decrepit or needs a new roof, the chairman ("Father of the Ermita") of the board of directors distributes in a fair manner the necessary workloads and material furnishings among the individual members of the cooperative. Every one of them strives without fail to supply his part of the effort, because he who does not care to do it would lose his right for a burial inside the ermita. Instead, he would be buried like a stranger who accidentally died in the vicinity, in a grave in the open air near the ermita and without its protection—a hard lot!

The souls who live in an ermita have a general assembly on All Souls' Day—the only day during the year when the ermita is not used as sleeping quarters by strangers traveling through. On this day the souls also visit the huts of their living relatives who put food and cigars on the home altar. Even though the souls are actually unable to use these items, they enjoy the smell of the delicacies and leave highly delighted. Thus, the souls lead a happy and contented traveling existence until they have repeated all the trips and thus satisfied their obligations to Tzuultaq'a.

After this, they must give an accounting before the Christian god and atone for their sins. Since the Indians imagine the Christian god as a white person, they suspect that he runs a ranch in the hereafter similar to those that the Europeans own in the Alta Verapaz. For that reason the Indians believe that they have to do the same kind of work in the next world as on earth (cutting down trees, doing fieldwork, cleaning, and so forth) until they have worked off their debt.

In contrast to the earthly ranches, where they never see the day when they have paid off all advances, they hope for a better deal in the next world. There, sooner or later, they would be rid of their debts and would be allowed to listen on the porch as the angels inside the house of God play for him on their celestial instruments (violins, guitars, and harps). The Indian is not so bold as to think he would be allowed inside the house of the Christian god. Here on earth he sees that the white man who visits a neighboring planter is

---

* These splotches of blood on posts and beams are not washed off and I had noticed them frequently, but no Indian had given me an explanation of their meaning. It wasn't until the twelfth year of my sojourn in Central America that an accident brought me the answer to the puzzle—an indication of how difficult it is to find explanations for such things.

led into the living room, while the Indian must stay on the porch or at most come into the kitchen. He thinks it will be the same in heaven since the Christian god is the god of the white people.

The Indian, however, is content; it appears quite proper that the god of the whites treats them somewhat better than the Indians. Similarly, he is convinced that Tzuultaq'a is only concerned with Indians, since they alone turn to him. The foreigners are not concerned with Tzuultaq'a, the Master of the Useful Plants. Consequently, when a foreigner wants to sow a cornfield, the *alcalde* (prayermaker) of the ranch feels obligated to offer the necessary prayers and sacrifices as a silent representation for the European planter.

The foregoing is the viewpoint of Q'eqchi' Indians who carry on the old traditions and live far from the centers of civilization. The urban Indians have become almost totally converted to Christianity, insofar as pure Christianity can ex-ist in a mixed population that is contaminated by all sorts of superstitions. A lot of variation can be found between the extremes. However strong the pagan element may be in the religious views of the Indians, it certainly does not disturb the religious peace in their hearts, even if the true peace cannot be found in them.

Notes

1. Ladinos are Westernized Spanish-speaking Latin Americans or persons of mixed European and American Indian ancestry.
2. Sapper misidentified the *ichb'olay* as *Crotalus horridus*, the genus commonly known as rattlesnake. *Ichb'olay* (*barba amarilla*, fer-de-lance) is *Bothrops asper*.
3. Sapper used "Master," but this is a female deity.
4. "Nagualism" refers to the belief that certain people can transform into an animal, in whose form they may become malevolent.
5. Sapper used the word *ánum* for "soul" in the original; in Spanish, however, "soul" is *ánima* or *alma*.

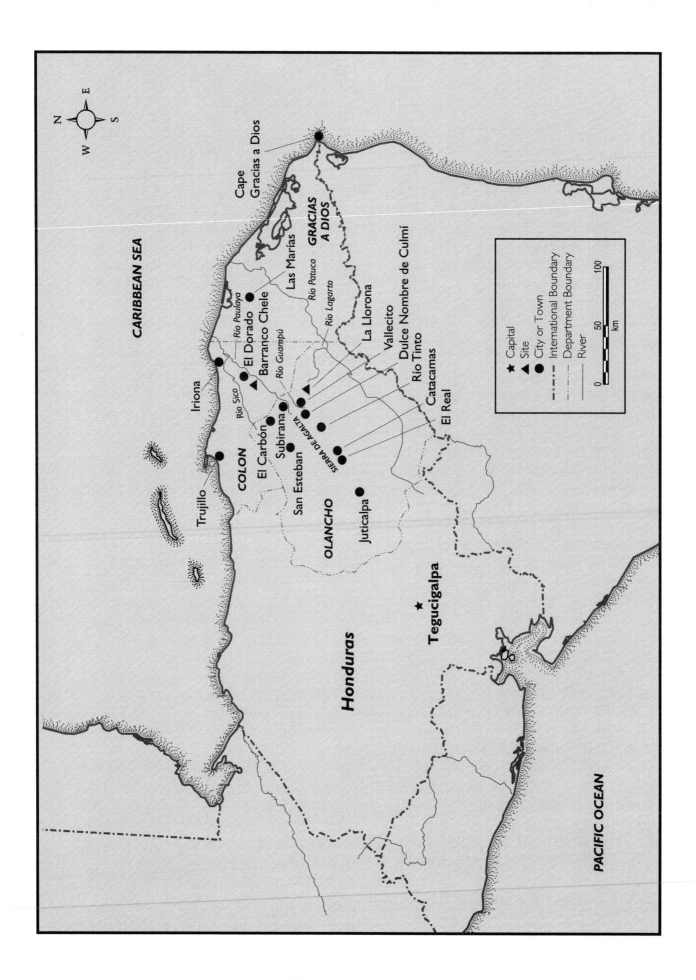

CHAPTER 5

The Payas of Honduras

Karl Sapper

Originally published as
"Die Payas in Honduras"
Globus 75(1899):80–83
Braunschweig: Druck und Verlag von Friedrich Vieweg und Sohn

COMMENTARY I

The problems (rapid population growth, environmental degradation, increasing crime, and a weak position in a global economy) currently facing the people of Honduras were not the major national concerns at the end of the nineteenth century. Sapper's report suggests, however, that the Pech (formerly called the Paya) did face issues in the 1890s with which they continue to struggle. These revolve around maintaining a meaningfully distinct cultural identity, something particularly difficult for such a small group, who numbered fewer than a thousand in 1898 and number about twenty-five hundred now. Some of Sapper's observations during his visits with the Pech in the 1890s reflect fundamental characteristics of the present situation. My observations are based on experience living and working in Pech communities from 1992 to 1997 while directing archaeological projects in eastern Honduras.

The "policy of withdrawal" that Sapper described is perhaps the most salient and pronounced characteristic of Pech life, a policy directing quotidian life in both rhetoric and practice, tempered somewhat by ideological ties with the Christian ladino population. Culmí, the Pech village visited by Sapper, is no longer a Pech town, others having sprung up farther east as the ladino population advanced from the west. Sapper notes that the Pech resisted intrusion since colonial times, and they continue to do so in many ways. In 1992, the Pech talked of celebrating five hundred years of resistance, a phrase popularized in indigenous communities throughout the New World during the 500th anniversary of Columbus' first voyage, and one that seemed to resonate particularly with the Pech. Through the "policy of withdrawal" the Pech continue their resistance.

At present, the Pech are struggling to maintain traditional elements of their culture, including the language, which were not in danger in Sapper's time. The Pech perceive the loss of their language as the greatest single threat to the traditional culture. This is a recurring topic of conversation in daily life and especially at political gatherings. Most Pech understand the traditional language, although children often respond in Spanish. The majority of households conduct everyday discourse in Spanish. I did not meet any Pech who could not speak Spanish fluently. The type of government-supplied Spanish-speaking teacher that Sapper mentioned "who does his level best to wipe out the memory of the language and the other peculiarities of the tribe" has, unfortunately, not completely disappeared, even though the intent is no longer there. Although many Pech schools have Pech teachers, community leaders in the village of Subirana estimated in 1994 that only one in five ever taught in the indigenous tongue. The rhetoric about the importance of preserving the language is strong, but the practice lags. In 1997, initiatives were made to teach more classes in the Pech language.

Most of the Pech participate in the Christian tradition. This is perhaps the area in which the greatest ties to the ladino population are felt. Sapper noted that the Pech had houses in the village of Culmí only in order to attend church and that many came on Saturday night and left after Mass. This same phenomenon continues to be manifested in other ways, with a certain amount of the interaction with the non-Pech community prompted by prosaic logistical concerns related to religious life. Now, the *cultos* (traveling evangelical groups) that hold revivals periodically in isolated communities are growing in popularity among the Pech.

While the Christian ideology is strong and the desire to participate in that tradition overrides the prevailing tendency towards segregation, the traditional cosmovision and legends have not disappeared. As with many indigenous groups, the two traditions are blended to some degree. For instance, healing is often accomplished in traditional ways, especially in cases of snakebite. Pech still have *curanderos* (medicine men). On a recent archaeological survey in the jungles of eastern Honduras, the Pech members of the team demanded that a curandero accompany us, primarily to prepare an herbal cure for snakebite. Traditional medicine is usually herbal, involving the preparation of teas and other liquids from a variety of local grasses, weeds, and other plants. I did not observe the exorcisms or hypnosis that Sapper mentions. Western medicine is used extensively also, although its use is constrained by availability and cost. In cases of extreme illness not associated with snakebite, a doctor or other specialist trained in western medicine is usually sought.

Other concerns demand a degree of interaction, of course, primarily economic in nature. In Subirana, for instance, the majority of vehicles that drive the last 5 km from the main road to the village come during the coffee harvest. Non-economic interaction is often tense. According to statistics gathered by the Honduran Institute of Anthropology and History in 1994, violence between Pech and ladinos is a leading cause of death among young Pech men.

Political organization among the Pech has changed since Sapper's visit. In 1985, the Pech organized the dispersed villages into a single political entity, the Federación de Tribus Pech de Honduras (FETRIPH), to deal with issues of health, education, land tenure, and economic activities. This organization superseded the traditional system of *caciques* (headmen), who were autonomous on a village level, with no real articulation with the caciques of other villages. FETRIPH is a democratic organization and is believed to be more effective in dealing with the threats from non-Pech entities, particularly the timber companies and the ladino population, which continues migrating into the area at an increasing rate.

Traditional economic and subsistence activities included an extensive utilization of forest resources, with hunting and fishing forming an important part of the village economy. Traditional lifeways also included the cultivation of root crops and other edible and medicinal plants. Today, subsistence activities are dominated by the farming of corn, beans, manioc,

sugarcane, and coffee and are indistinguishable from those of the non-Pech in the area. Hunting and fishing are now activities that require a special trip into the forest, and fewer people participate as intensively as before; however the Pech continue these activities more frequently than the non-Pech populations and are renowned for their success. *Sasal*, the manioc bread that Sapper mentions, continues to be important and is now appreciated by much of the ladino population. (Dennis Holt mentions its being prepared in Vallecito during his 1997 visit.) Sapper also notes the preference for manioc over corn, a preference evident today that has prehistoric origins, reflecting the essentially non-Mesoamerican nature of the prehistoric as well as modern groups in the Atlantic watershed of Central America.

Sapper discusses the collection of metates for household use from archaeological sites. Such collecting is still done, although the sites mentioned have been depleted and other sites have replaced them. This ongoing tradition reflects the increasing danger to the cultural resources of eastern Honduras as more immigrants arrive. The practice of using archaeological metates is not limited to the Pech.

Sapper's prediction that "the complete disappearance of the tribe has to be expected within not too long a time" has not come to pass, and the language and other attributes that make the Pech unique survive. The struggle to preserve this identity continues in a manner similar to that noted by Sapper. In addition to the forces of dislocation and assimilation that have threatened them in the past, the Pech are now facing the challenge of articulating a traditional lifeway emphasizing forest resources within the national/global economy, a challenge also faced by other groups. The next hundred years will undoubtedly be critical. The current consciousness raising and efforts at cultural revival offer hope that a reexamination of the situation at the end of the twenty-first century will show Sapper's pessimism to be unwarranted.

–*Christopher Taylor Begley*

COMMENTARY 2

My experience with the Pech (formerly Paya) people began in 1974, when, as a research assistant under a National Science Foundation grant, I visited the area around Dulce Nombre de Culmí to assess the current status of their language and to gather linguistic materials.

There are three principal Pech settlements, all of them in the northern part of the Department of Olancho: Vallecito, which is situated in the foothills of the Sierra de Agalta about 5 km northeast of the town of Dulce Nombre de Culmí; Marañones, or Pueblo Nuevo Subirana, or Kahã Wayka (New Town), which lies about 15 km north of Culmí, also in the Sierra de Agalta foothills; and El Carbón (originally Santa María del Carbón), which is located near the Quebrada Agua Amarilla in a higher mountain valley in the upper Río Sico watershed, some 35 km north of Culmí and about 30 km northeast of the town of San Esteban. Vallecito and Marañones each had between 120 and 150 inhabitants in 1975. El Carbón was reported at that time to be approximately twice as large. A number of smaller Pech settlements are scattered about the mountains and valleys of the upper Río Guampú watershed in northern Olancho; the largest of these includes only a few families and probably not more than 40 individuals. A small settlement (Las Marías) on the Río Platano in the Department of Gracias a Dios, which was once a purely Pech community, has become a mixed community of Pech and Mískito people from the nearby coastal areas during the last thirty years or so.

Dulce Nombre de Culmí, once the largest Pech settlement in the entire Río Guampú watershed, was gradually evacuated by the Pech beginning in the 1950s, until by 1974 only a single Pech family remained. Early in 1997, this last Pech family left Culmí and retired to Vallecito. Over all, this exodus seems to have been the result of the influx of large numbers of ladino people into Culmí, an immigration brought about by the increased commercial exploitation of the forest resources of the area, including the con-struction and operation of a number of sawmills and a plywood factory. In recent years, this activity has abated substantially. Despite the near total absence of Pech inhabitants in Culmí over the last forty years, the town has continued to serve as the religious center for the Pech people, much as Sapper reports it to have done at the time of his visit.

The continued use of a previously occupied community as a religious center seems to have been a widespread state of affairs among peoples of Mesoamerica and nearby regions. Ernesto Cardenal refers to this in his poem "Las ciudades perdidas." Speaking of the Maya, he says, "Their cities were made up of temples, and they lived out in the country, among fields and palm-trees and papayas" (1979: 140–143). I have observed a similar situation among the Huichol in northern Jalisco, Mexico. The small basilica in the plaza of Culmí is considered by the Pech to be their own special church, since it was one of them who experienced the vision on which the Spanish part of the town's name is based. Accordingly, the Pech long ago took on the perennial responsibility of cleaning and maintaining the basilica building and grounds.

Pech language and culture were apparently much more widely distributed throughout northeastern Honduras at the time of first Spanish contact in the early sixteenth century, probably extending along the Caribbean coast from the longitude of the present-day town of Trujillo in the west (the eastern border of Tol territory) all the way to Cape Gracias a Dios in the east and as far inland as the upper Río Patuca.

Pech, the northernmost of the Chibchan family of languages, is still spoken in the Honduran departments of Olancho and Colón by perhaps 600 speakers, most of them adults more than 20 years of age. During the early 1970s, principally through the efforts of Ezequiel Martínez, the schoolteacher in Pueblo Nuevo Subirana, a movement was begun to teach Pech to young children. By the 1980s, with the help of educators and anthropologists and partly due to the instigation of the Federación de Tribus Pech de Honduras (mentioned by Christopher Taylor Begley in commentary 1), this had developed into the Pech Bilingual Education Project at the Escuela Superior del Profesorado "Francisco Morazán" in Tegucigalpa.

During the last few years, the Honduran Ministry of Education, through its Programa para el Mejoramiento de la Educación Básica (PROMEB) and its subagency Programa Nacional de Educación para las Etnias Autóctonas y Afroantillanas de Honduras (PRONEEAAH), has begun to create bilingual educational materials for the Pech. A small orthography textbook and a reading primer have already been produced and are now in use in the three principal Pech settlements. A monolingual Pech dictionary is now being developed by a team made up of Blas López Catalán of Santa María del Carbón; Prudencio García, a Honduran linguist; and Ezequiel Martínez. I am serving as International Consultant for this project, which is for me both an honor and a privilege. Additionally, I am currently developing a reference grammar of the language in Spanish, which will aid developers of programs and materials and teachers in the Pech bilingual education program.

In the future I hope to be involved in the creation of additional literacy materials for the Pech people in their own language. Recently, Lázaro Flores, a Honduran anthropologist, and Wendy Griffin, a researcher from the United States, have gathered a number of folkloric texts in Spanish, some of which have been published in their book *Dioses, héroes y hombres en el universo mítico pech* (1991). Such texts, in the original language, could serve the important function of preserving some part of the Pech oral literary tradition, as well as stimulating new literary production, both oral and written, among current speakers. It seems that the continued existence of the language as a viable instrument of communication depends on the success of such efforts at revitalization and transmission to younger people. Without such success, however, the language would probably be destined for extinction sometime in this century.

As a final note, I returned to Vallecito during the summer of 1997 to visit with my informants from the 1970s, all of whom are still living and in good health. While there, I was able to observe the preparation and to participate again in the consumption of *sasal*, the national dish of the Pech made of fermented manioc, which is still prepared exactly as Sapper describes it in his account.

–*Dennis Holt*

The Payas of Honduras

The Indian tribes of Honduras are represented less in the history of Middle America than the more civilized people of the Maya family in Yucatán, Guatemala, and Chiapas, who were united into larger ordered state societies. Not even the names of some of the Honduran Indian groups have come down to us. That is the case with the Payas, who reside in the eastern part of the country and presumably also did so at the time of the conquest.

We do know that Diego López de Salcedo was the cause of many cruelties against the native Indians around the year 1528. After the founding of Xuticalpa (Juticalpa) by Alonso Ortiz, the Indians began to rebel and to retire into the inaccessible virgin forest to avoid working in the numerous gold- panning operations of the region. In 1531, however, Ortiz was able to calm them and persuade them to remain.

Then again in 1531, the Indians in the vicinity of Trujillo, who presumably also belonged to the Paya tribe, rebelled, taking advantage of the struggle between the two governors, Cerezeda and Herrera. Under the leadership of their cacique Picecura, they fled into the woods, and Vasco de Herrera was unable to induce them to return.

Later on one looks in vain in the annals of history for detailed reports about the fate of the Payas. Without doubt, they continued to follow their policy of withdrawal as they remained loyal to their beliefs. In the course of time their numbers have diminished more and more, and only scarce remains of pure Payas have survived into our century. The survivors were converted to Christianity around the middle of the nineteenth century by the Spanish missionary Manuel de Subirana and were made to speak Spanish.

Subirana gathered a large segment of the Payas into the little village of Culmí, where in 1861 he also built a church. He changed the name of the village to "Dulce Nombre," following the custom of the earlier missionaries who tried in that way to extinguish the memory of the heathen past. The same thing happened here as with similar name changes in Guatemala, where the Indians accepted the new Spanish name, but the overall population continued to use the old name. Thus, even today, one hears the old name Culmí more frequently than the official name of Dulce Nombre. Culmí is still the main village of the Payas and, since my travel in 1898 took me into that region anyhow, I did not want to miss finding out about this village which a European has rarely visited. I wandered from Catacamas with three Q'eqchi' Indians in a northeasterly direction through hilly country, traveling partly through savannas, partly through pine forests.

Towards the evening of 11 March we came to the little village of Río Tinto which is located in a lovely clearing of the pine forest. The following evening we found a similarly located village in a clearing of the

Pech Glossary

Native word	Spelling in original	Spanish	English
aña (ava, eca)	aña (ava, eca)		Pronoun, 3rd pers. sing.
aun	aun	maiz	Corn
avuayó	avuayó	mano	Rounded grinding stone used with a metate
chaá	chaá	sasal	Steamed manioc tamale, bread
hoo'tuk (Q'eqchi')	hootuc		200 (5 x 40)
isacá	isacá	frijoles	Beans
pratá	pratá	plátano grande	Large plantain
sancvuá	sancvuá	guineos	Small bananas
sayú	sayú	metate	Grinding stone; lower stone against which the mano is rolled
séri	séri	olla grande	Large cooking pot
tiquimijá	tiquimijá	tuno	Broad band placed across chest to aid in carrying load on back
tortíyaha	tortíyaha	tortillas	Tortillas, corn cakes
totopostehá	totopostehá	totoposte	Tortilla prepared to last several months
yóvra	yóvra	yuca	Manioc (*Manihot utilissima*)

forest, the object of our trip, Culmí. We were able to stay with one of the few locally resident mestizo families, and on the first evening I was able to walk around the village in company of a locally acquainted Honduran. There seemed to be nothing unusual, since the Indians were forced to set up their houses in a straight line street pattern. The white painted church with its small bell tower stands on the small village square; next to it is the house of the priest, which is lived in only rarely. Across from the church is the small town hall. The rest of the square is bordered by thatch-roofed private residences. The majority of the small village squares in the country look exactly the same.

At other villages, even very small ones, during this hour of the evening one sees people moving about, taking care of their obligations. Firelight escapes the houses through cracks; one hears sounds of people and animals. Here in Culmí, however, everything was quiet and silent at the square, all houses were closed; the impression was as if the entire village had died out. The Payas have their regular homes in dispersed small buildings outside the village. Everyone also has his own house within the village but lives in it only for their Sunday visit to the church. They come into town Saturday night and leave again on Sunday night or Monday morning. During the week almost all the houses stand empty. A few are lived in on account of schoolchildren. Dulce Nombre has a government-supported schoolmaster who does his level best to wipe out the memory of the language and the other peculiarities of the tribe.

Currently, the situation in the village is such that the Payas speak their mother tongue as well as more or less proper Spanish; but only the youth of the village are able to read or write. The Payas who live outside Culmí speak only very broken Spanish, as I found out on my later trip to the little Paya village of Santa María del Real[1] on the Río Sico.

The communal government in Culmí is exactly like that in other Honduran villages. In the first place, the Indians listen to the advice of one of their own, who occupies a leading role among them and is called their *gobernador* (governor; political chief). Currently, this position is occupied by don Leonardo Duarte, a friendly, intelligent Indian whom I met during my visit to Culmí.

When I repeated my wanderings through the village on Sunday morning, I observed some life in the streets and houses. Here and there one saw a Paya family move in with children and all. An Indian stood on the bell tower and rang the bell; next to him some youngsters with drums and flutes invited people to prayers with their music. Since the door to the church was wide open, I went into the empty interior without seeing anything noteworthy there. The miracle-working picture of the Virgin, the pride of Culmí, was still locked in its shrine.

Soon after I left the church, its interior began to fill with believers, the majority of whom were women, just as one can observe in Europe. The Paya women are dressed just like the mestizo women. Later on I met a Paya woman near Trujillo who wore men's pants, but this deviation from the norm can be easily explained by the infestation of ticks, against which women's skirts are no protection.

After the religious services, the men assembled in the priest's house for the purpose of an election. It appeared that they had a difficult time deciding upon a person to be the new *regidor* (alderman or magistrate), because they remained for more than four hours in consultation. After the election, the schoolteacher and community scribe or recorder, don Gregorio Duarte, had me stand up and introduced me to the assembly. He explained the reason for my visit and read the letter of commendation from the president of the state, don Policarpo Bonilla. While the letter circulated among the few Paya Indians who could read, I had time to observe the assembled people more closely. Around on the walls of the large room sat about forty Indians with some mestizos; about twenty other Payas had taken seats around a long table in the middle of the room, where I also was seated.

The many Indians watched me with unconcealed curiosity, while I let my eyes move about just as curiously. The clothing of these men did not vary much from that of the ladinos, except that the Payas clothed themselves exclusively in white cotton fabrics, as do the majority of Middle American Indians who live in a hot or even moderate climate. A red cotton ribbon secures their pants; leather sandals and a straw hat complete their outfit. The people are of small or medium stature; one may guess an average height of 155 cm (about 61 inches). They are noticeably broad shouldered; a broad skull with strongly protruding cheekbones rests on a surprisingly short neck. Their very straight black hair is cut half length; their skin color is a rather light brown. The mouth is large; the face often is ugly, especially among those Indians who suffer from a skin malady known as *tiña* or *catavi* (a ringworm infection of the scalp) and whose facial skin is almost completely blue. Among the Payas one can observe frequently a tendency to big abdomens, something rare among the Indians of Guatemala. The Paya women are definitely more attractive than the men, as their heads and shoulders are less broad. Among several younger female Indians I observed rather pretty faces.

After my letter of introduction was returned to me, the Indians let me know their willingness

TABLE 5.1
Conjugation of the verb "to sow" in Paya

Present

I sow my cornfield	tas tixbá ta aská
You sow your cornfield	pa tixkú pi aská
He sows his cornfield	aña tixvá a aská
We sow our cornfield	ntásña atizbarvá nt aská
You sow your cornfield	acvuá tixcvuá pix aská
They sow their cornfield	ek'aña tixquervá a aská

Perfect

I have sown my cornfield	quitasmá tixbava ta aská
You have sown your cornfield	pa vá tixkrí pi aská
He has sown his cornfield	aña tixki a aská
We have sown our cornfield	ntásña tixbarí nt aská
You have sown your cornfield	acvuá a tixchejri pix aská
They have sown their cornfield	ek'áña a tixquerí a aská

Future

I will/go to sow my cornfield	tas avayú a tixbá ta aská
You will sow your cornfield	pa va atixcu pia (pi) aská
He will sow his cornfield	aña tixpiá a aská
We will sow our cornfield	ntasña a tixparpiá nt aská
You will sow your cornfield	acvuá tixquerpiá pix aská
They will sow their cornfield	ek'aña tixquerpia a aská

to give me information. I first asked about the route from Culmí northward and was given the information quickly, even though the entire assembly took part in that discussion, mostly in their Indian language and thus unintelligible to me. When I began to ask about the Paya language, the majority of the Indians got bored and left the room. The few, mostly older, Payas who remained along with their leader, don Leonardo Duarte, became so tired after a short while from their unaccustomed concentration that I could find out nothing more from them.

It is reasonably easy to get simple vocabularies from the Indians, but in contrast it is very difficult, in a short span of time, to find out any useful grammatical material. It was grammatical information that I was most interested in, since the schoolteacher, don Gregorio Duarte, had earlier collected a rather extensive vocabulary of the language and had published it in Alberto Membreño's *Hondureñismos* (1897). Despite all my efforts, I succeeded in recording only a few incomplete conjugations. I publish here (table 5.1) the most complete one, since we are dealing with a language that

Table 5.2

Numbering systems in Middle American languages

	Paya (Honduras)	Jicaque (Honduras)	Pipil (San Agustín Acasaguastlán, Guatemala)
1	as	paní	ce
2	poc	máta	úmi
3	mai	condo	yéi
4	caa	diurupána	návui
5	aúnqui	comasofuí	mácuil
6	séra	-	chicvuás
7	tavuá	-	chicúmi (5+2)
8	óva	-	chicvuey (5+3)
9	tax	-	chicvuávi (5+4)
10	úca	comasfó	matácti
11	uca ras (10+1)	-	-
12	ucarapoc (10+2)	-	-
13	ucaramai	-	-
14	ucaracaa	-	-
15	ucaraaunqui (10+5)	-	coxtuli
20	vuauca	chinampani	cempúal
21	vuaucaras (20+1)	-	
22	vuaucarapoc (20+2)	-	
30	mai tup	-	-
40	ísca (2 x 20)	chinammates (2x20)	umpúal
41	íscar as (40+1)	-	
50	íscar uca (40+10)	-	
60	iscar vuaucau (40+20)	chinamcontes (3 x 20)	yejpuáli (3 x 20)
70	íscar mai tup (40+30)	-	
80	íscar tapac poc (2 x 40)	chinamyurupá (4 x 20)	návuipuáli (4 x 20)
90	íscapoc a ruca (80+10)	-	-
100	íspoc	chinamcomasofuí (5 x 20)	macouipuáli (5 x 20)

up to now has been totally unknown.[2]

Instead of placing the object at the end of the sentence, it is frequently put in front of the verb (that is, between the personal pronoun and the verb). The prefix of an "a" in front of the word for time, as observed at numerous places, does not seem necessary here, but this could be clarified only with a larger number of examples. The pronunciation is also very uncertain; thus one hears for the pronoun of the third person singular *aña*

as well as *ava*, and also *eca*, and so on.

The Paya language is differentiated from all Indian languages of Middle America that I know in its vocabulary, as well as in the inflection/conjugation of its verbs. Surprising to me was the similar sound of the second-person singular possessive pronoun in Paya and in Jicaque. In Jicaque one says, "You sow your cornfield" (*ya can sín pi tzitzi*) versus "I sow my cornfield" (*min zin nan tzitzi*).

Of special interest in the Paya language are the words for numbers insofar as they appear to indicate a system based on forty, which in other Middle American languages has only an occasional use (for example, 200 in Q'eqchi' = *hoo'tuk* = 5 x 40). Usually the vigesimal system dominates Middle American Indian languages, which is explained by the number of fingers and toes, just as five, the number of fingers on one hand, forms a clearly apparent subdivision in Nahuatl and in Jicaque (see table 5.2). To find an explanation for a forty-based system would be difficult since it would be too farfetched to add together the number of fingers and toes of a man and woman (as representing a higher natural unity in the household of nature).

When I became aware that for the time being little more about their language would be forthcoming from the Indians, I began to ask them about their habits and customs. Naturally, I did not get any real answer; I was assured that they had already discontinued all old customs and that they lived just like the mestizos. With regard to their life-style, they told me that their main foods were manioc and corn, predominantly the former. It is noteworthy that the Jicaques and the tribes of eastern Nicaragua also prefer manioc as their basic food, while it is rather unimportant for the tribes of the Maya area.

The Payas plant the type of manioc (*yóvra*) that is not poisonous (*Manihot utilissima*) and mill it with the mano (*avuayó*) or the metate (*sayú*) as if it were corn. Then they wrap up the manioc paste in leaves in order to steam it (*sasal* in Spanish, *chaá* in Paya) in large ceramic vessels (*séri*). Originally they understood only how to use corn (*aun*) to make tamales, pozole, pinole, and atole, just like the Jicaques. Only recently have they learned to make tortillas that are like these in the Maya and Aztec areas and among the mestizos. For this reason they do not have their own word for them (*tortíyaha*). Formerly, they did not know the dried long-term corn cake and for that reason they now use the Nahuatl name (*totoposte*) that is used in the Spanish dialect of Middle America, but with an ending current in their language (*totopostehá*). Besides manioc and corn, beans (*isacá*) and bananas play a major role in their diet—the large *plátanos* (*pratá*), as well as the small *guineos* (*sancvuá*).

The present Payas no longer know how to make metates, but the neighboring Jicaques still make them from hard stones of large recently erupted materials. The Payas find their metates in old ruins, one of which is about 15 leagues east of Culmí on the Río Lagarto near the La Llorona (formerly Cuesta de Llorona). A second, evidently more important place of ruins is located along the trail from Culmí to Iriona on the Río Paulaya at Barranco Chele (formerly El Barranco) near El Dorado. It is said that a number of stone idols have been found at the El Barranco ruins.

To see one of these metates I went with don Leonardo Duarte and some other Indians into a Paya house and observed that the three-legged metate was adorned with an animal head; the mano was long and cylindrical. The house was a hut of almost square ground plan; the roof was covered with grass; the wall of wood sticks was extended about one foot beyond the corner posts. The interior furnishings were extremely simple. Besides the rack for the metate, I observed only the fireplace and the bed. The bed was a simple wooden rack covered with *tuno*,[3] a rubber-rich tree bark that is made soft by beating; it is also used by the Payas as a blanket.

Despite the fact that the Payas clothe themselves exclusively in cotton materials these days, it is probable that earlier they wore bark clothing, as did the neighboring Jicaques just a few decades ago and as some of the eastern Nicaragua Indians still do. In this respect, as well as by their life-style, they stand in definite contrast to the tribes of the Aztec and Maya families.

After the visit to this house, Leonardo Duarte and a number of Payas went with me to enjoy the well-earned brandy and also to see my Q'eqchi' porters, whose carrying racks (*cacastes*), umbrellas (*suyacales*), and carrying straps (*mecapales*) were of great interest to the Payas. They themselves are no longer able to carry heavy loads nor do they carry their burden with a strap over the head as the Indians of Guatemala do. Rather, they use a broad *tuno* (*tiquimijá*) across the chest in order to carry the load on their back.

Fairly soon the Payas bade me good-bye, and when I left the village the following morning to continue my trip, most of the houses were already empty again. The village schoolmaster accompanied me for a stretch and shared on this occasion his observations on the customs of the Payas.

The Payas pay great attention to their dreams, similar to the Indians of Guatemala. If a sick person dreams of someone, they believe that person is the cause of the illness, that he/she had enchanted or bewitched the sick person. In former times they tried to kill this supposed author of the illness; but more recently this custom, under the strong control of the government, has been abandoned.

The Payas also have their special doctors who, as in other Indian tribes, probably resort frequently to incantations of exorcism and influence by hypnosis. They have, of course, many medicines from plants that are supposed to give good results. If the sickness gets dangerous, they try to scare death away by shooting some guns. Formerly, they used to fire guns at burials also and to have food and personal tools accompany the deceased. For some years now the schoolmaster has disabused them of these customs. The house of the deceased is vacated and destroyed.

Polygamy has been discontinued since the introduction of Christianity. A wife is acquired by purchase. A man can also demand the child of a pregnant woman if it turns out to be a girl, but he must then support the mother as well as the child. At weddings, old dances are held, but strangers may not see them. Even the schoolmaster in Culmí, who has lived for many years among the Payas, has never seen these dances. The musical instruments are pipes and drums. A fermented drink is made of manioc, which the Payas imbibe in quantity at festive occasions. The Payas are not acquainted with song any more than the majority of other Middle American Indians. The use of bows and arrows is almost completely abandoned; blowguns are used for smaller birds only; only guns are used for hunting; for fishing, only fishing rods or harpoons are used, no nets.

The number of Payas at the present time is very small. In Culmí 385 souls have been counted; in the little village of El Carbón there are supposed to be 300 Payas; in Santa María on the Río Sico, maybe another 50; in the settlement Guarascá on the Río Alazán and on the Río Paulaya, perhaps 30 more in each place. Thus, the total number of Payas just barely surpasses 800! At present, the Payas strongly resist marriage with mixed-blood people; but in spite of this, the complete disappearance of the tribe has to be expected within the not too distant future. In any case, the language will disappear even sooner, as will be the case with the neighboring Jicaques. Even now the Indian language among the Lencas in southwestern Honduras is spoken only in a few villages by a few older persons, even though the number of pure-blooded Indians there is still quite considerable.

Thus, the Indians of the interior stand in a rather noteworthy contrast to the tribes of the Honduran northern coast. The latter (Garifuna and Zambos) have maintained their language, but can no longer be somatically counted among the Indians, since they have intermingled with blacks for generations and physically more closely resemble blacks rather than pure Indians. The admixture of Indian blood does show up vis-à-vis pure-blooded blacks in smaller bodies and other physiognomic differences.

Notes

1. This is a small hamlet on the bank of the Río Sico whose correct name is Santa María or Toyaco according to Lanza et al. 1992:11.

2. Sapper used "orthography based on Stoll"; we follow current linguistic practice.

3. Sapper used the word *tuno* to refer to both the material and the object made from it.

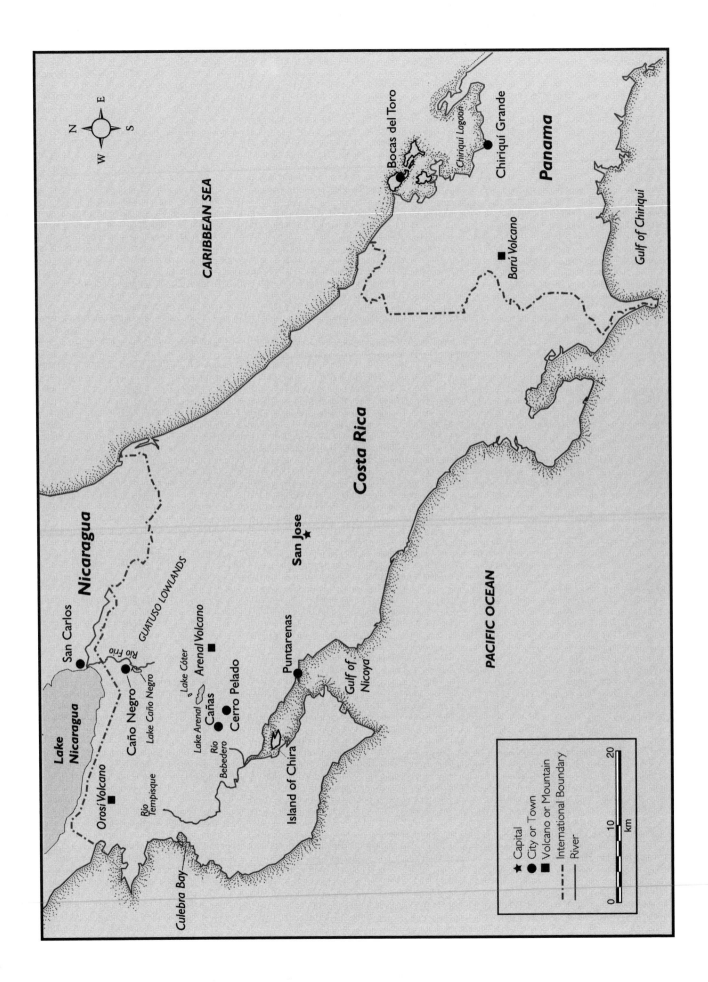

CHAPTER 6

A Visit with the Guatusos of Costa Rica

Karl Sapper

Originally published as
"Ein Besuch bei den Guatusos in Costarica"
Globus 76(1899):348-353
Braunschweig: Druck und Verlag von Friedrich Vieweg und Sohn

Commentary

In 1899 Karl Sapper and his porter walked from the Pacific coast of Costa Rica to the Continental Divide and down into the Atlantic drainage to visit the Guatuso Indians. It took them six days, traveling "slowly and observantly" as they preferred. Eighty-six years later, in 1985, driving along approximately the same route, it took us slightly more than six hours, but I must admit we missed many details that Sapper would have noted. Sadly, most of the tropical forest seen and enjoyed by Sapper is gone. I was directing an archaeological research project in the Arenal area of Costa Rica, only 20 km south of the Guatusos. We, too, wanted to talk with the Guatusos and see how they lived.

We thought we were close to the first Guatuso village, so we pulled over and asked a man walking along the roadside where it was. He replied in flawless Spanish "just up the road a bit" and said he was going there and would be glad to show us, and so we gave him a ride. I asked him if he knew any Guatusos and to our surprise he said he was Guatuso. We had not a clue from his dress or language. Also surprising was his answer to a question regarding from where he was coming. From San Jose, he said, where he studied computer science at the national university.

Sapper's principal reason for visiting the Guatusos was their lack of acculturation, and I am certain he would be astounded at the changes. The architecture has changed from the huge roofs that housed dozens of families to individual houses that now contain single extended families. What were thatch roofs are now (much hotter) galvanized iron, and all the houses have walls. Many have electricity, which facilitates radio, television, and an occasional telephone, all of which whet the soaring appetite for material objects among the young. Another great change is the rever-sal in language: during Sapper's visit, all were fluent in Guatuso and their Spanish was halting. Now it is difficult to find someone who knows much Guatuso. Their clothing has also changed completely, from the mainly breechcloths of Sapper's day to the exclusively western clothing of today.

On the other hand, there is some recognizable cultural continuity, particularly where it pertains to household activities. The male heads of households still fish and hunt and are away often during the day-time (although sometimes for longer periods when they hold distant jobs). The Guatusos sleep in hammocks under mosquito nets much as in the past. They cook on elevated hearths in kitchens and in special small structures outside. They ferment manioc, bananas, *pejibaye* (fruit of the palm tree, *Bactris gasipaes*), or corn into a mildly alcoholic drink called *chicha*. The men use machetes, once made of a tropical hardwood and now of steel. Their dietary staples are still manioc, bananas, pejibaye, and corn, but other such Western items as canned tuna, sodas, and distilled drinks have been added.

Sapper visited the Guatusos when they were at an extreme low point. They had been defeated by well-armed Nicaraguan troops, and he predicted that they would soon die out. He was wrong, as they have adapted rapidly to their changing circumstances. We detected none of the physical or mental health problems that Sapper observed, and certainly no limitations on intellectual abilities, as exemplified by our university student guide. What has been lost without adequate documentation is the traditional culture, adaptation, language, religion, and worldview.

–Payson D. Sheets

A Visit with the Guatusos of Costa Rica

I arrived at the harbor of Punta Arenas (Puntarenas) on the soil of Costa Rica on 18 April 1899, after I had crossed the Isthmus of Chiriquí from Bocas del Toro via Chiriquí Grande and Calderas[1] and had climbed the Chiriquí (Barú) volcano at a height of 3670 m. From there I expected to undertake the rare trip to San Carlos on Lake Nicaragua and to become better acquainted with the Guatusos, an Indian tribe that appears to be the least acculturated tribe of Costa Rica. I therefore left Puntarenas on a small steamship at 6 A.M. on the 20th of April, and we crossed the Gulf of Nicoya in splendid weather toward the mouth of the Río Tempixque (Tempisque). We passed the island of Chira, which I knew well, in front of which several sailboats were anchored in order to load cedar, a main export article of Guanacaste province.

Around 9:30 A.M. we reached the mouth of the Río Tempisque, the main aquatic vein of Guanacaste, which crosses a low chalky mountain range shortly before flowing into the ocean. As soon as one has crossed this part of the rocky shoreline, mangrove thickets start on both sides. The water of the river is quite brackish here since the tide advances very far upriver. The small mail steamer can advance as far as the tide allows on the Tempisque and its main tributary, the Bebedero; for that reason the departure times depend on those of the tide.

We went up the Tempisque only a short stretch and then turned to the right; progress was slow on account of the movement of the river, but we arrived near noon at the village of Bebedero located at the confluence of two rather considerable rivers. From Bebedero I went on foot with my Indian porter, Sebastián Ical, on a gently rising plain in terrific heat, where mostly thorn bushes with few leaves grow. Among the poor shrubs a considerable number of large leafy trees have grown, the majority of which lose their leaves during the dry season. Large stretches of the road were completely without trees or shrubbery. The entire character of the vegetation seemed to indicate that this region must undergo a very intensive, long period of dryness. The frequent four-edged cereus forms confirmed this assumption. The large eight-edged cereus forms, such as are found in Guatemala, Honduras, and Nicaragua, as well as near the ocean in Costa Rica, were not present.

At the beginning of nighttime we reached the village of Cañas (90 m), from where we made a two-day excursion to the Cerro Pelado (720 m), which had mistakenly been advertised as a volcano. We continued our trip on 23 April to the Río Frío. A policeman on horseback was to lead us up to the last house of the barrio of Santa Rosa (hacienda of Julián Alvarado). This man charged a considerable amount for his services (4 pesos). He figured himself above the role of guide, however, and usually rode far ahead, although he waited for us at several road forks. I finally had to seriously remind him of his

Guatuso Glossary

Word	Spelling in Original	Spanish	English
carréjor	caresfóri		Type of dried creeper used to make fire
chiqui	chiqui	ahumador circular	Round sieve made of basket-weave fiber; container used to smoke food over a fire
chíu	chiyu		Clay pot
cólocóma	cóloco		Necklace
cotí pal	cutipala		Literally, "piece of chilamate," this is a band made of inner bark of chilamate (*Ficus* sp)
cucánhíya	cucanjiya	mastate	Mastate tree (Moraceae); its fine bark material is used to make various articles
cúfi	cujo	hamaca	Hammock
jélenh	jelico	taparrabo	Breechcloth
jerro	jerro		Carrying net
lhaca	sáca	hermano	Brother
lhafára	sabára	bramadera	"Whizzing wood" used in divining. "Lhafára" is the name of the daughter of the chief of the gods. The rattle or horn is used to communicate with her.
lhijílha	siís	colador	Guacales made into sieves by boring holes
macháro	macharo		Devil of the sky (generic name for eternal evil spirits as well as for people who upon dying are condemned and go to be punished by them in the place of punishment in the sky)
Oronhcaf	oronco		Proper name of the chief of devils of the sky
pupa	púpa	jícaro, jicara, guacal	Drinking cups or bowls made from the wood of from the jícaro tree (*Crescentia cujete*)
púrrunh	búru	tamal	Tamale
quirrílenh	quirili		Traditional woman's garment
quirrímun	quirumbun		Bottle gourds; fruit of the calabash tree (*Lagenaria siceraria* [Molina])
tali	tali	tambor	Drum (made of bitter cedar [*Cedrela mexicana* Roem.])
tóji	toji		Sun (god of all goodness to Guatusos)

duty, since I once almost made a wrong turn. All told, he was a harsh taskmaster, as are almost all riders or pedestrians without loads, so that my porter was in danger of becoming exhausted. We were, therefore, glad to get rid of this miserable man, so that the two of us could continue the trip in our usual manner, going slowly and observantly.

We spent the night at the hacienda of Julián Alvarado (660 m), which is in the region of the moist rain forest. For that reason it is well adapted at its altitude for the production of coffee. In fact, quite a bit of coffee that looks healthy has already been planted here; bananas and tobacco plants with light red blossoms are also raised.

At this hacienda starts the narrow but well-used pedestrian path, which leads in a northeasterly direction to the Río Frío through uninterrupted, extensive, and uninhabited virgin forests. This forest is fresh and green, but here not yet very dense. The undergrowth is not yet thickly developed, and quite a few leafy trees grow here. Soon one crosses the watershed (780 m) between the Atlantic and Pacific Oceans, and now the forest becomes much more luxuriant. It is richer with palms and tree ferns, as well as climbers and epiphytic plants that occupy hospitable trees and their branches. Our trip through this forest was a pleasure. Regardless of a few steep places and some stretches of bogs, it was not strenuous but full of natural beauty, especially at those places where rushing, clear mountain streams divide the thickets of the forest or where open stretches of water (Lake Cóter) can be seen in the midst of the dark green. Without special adventures we arrived around 9 A.M. on the 26th of April at the hamlet of Guatuso (about 60 m) on the Río Frío, where until recently the government of Costa Rica had maintained a military post. At this time only one government official takes care of order and respect for the frontier. The official took us hospitably to his house and procured for me at once an efficient guide, so that at midday I could begin to visit some nearby *palenques* (dwellings built of posts) of the Guatusos.

All of them are located in a southeasterly direction from the Comandancia Guatuso on the Río Frío, in part on the flat land, in part on the first of the mountainous hills. The nearest of these palenques is not even 2 km in a direct line from the Comandancia, while the most distant (Grecia) is about 12 km away. The diffusion of the Guatusos is therefore very limited, while Pittier's 1898 ethnographic map gave them a considerable area. Bishop Dr. Thiel had ascertained through informants during his fifth visit in 1896 that there were 267 souls: 133 men, 70 women, and 64 children. Their number may have diminished somewhat since then, but not by much. Their distribution is different, however, as two-fifths of their number currently live in the palenque Margarita, where the government until a short time ago had maintained a soldier (my guide Juan Paesano).

The path to the palenques is a bad footpath, rather overgrown and frequently crossed by fallen trees, which have to be climbed over unless one can crawl under them. The first palenque that we found was uninhabited. It consisted of two large houses with sloped roofs and half a house—a shed that had a roof inclined to one side only (figure 6.1).

The main house covered an area of 18 m per side. The ridge of the roof rests on three sturdy pillars consisting of round poles 40 cm in diameter. These pillars do not stand on the middle line of the house; thus the two roof inclinations are different from each other (20° and 35°). The ends of the roofs rest on five shorter pillars and reach down to 1 m above ground.

There is no wall. The roof is carefully covered by palm leaves and is supposed to be rather long lasting. (The construction of the remaining palenques is similar.) The dwellings at times consist of two half-houses next to each other, whose roofs at their upper ends are separated from each other by about one foot; they do not come together at a joint ridge.

The furnishing of this palenque is very simple and typical of the rest of them. One can see some hammocks made of woven *burillo* (fiber obtained from the dry trunk of plantain or banana trees) ropes with some wooden sticks put in the earth alongside of them. The man sleeps in the hammock (*cúfi*), while the woman sleeps alongside on the ground; the wooden sticks serve to prop up the mosquito net above them. At times there are wooden frames that rest on posts or are hung from

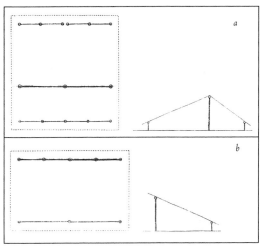

Figure 6.1 Structures at the first palenque: a, plan view and cross section of the main building; b, plan view and cross section of the half-house. Scale 1:400

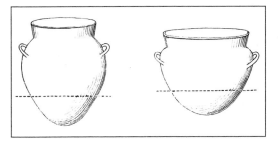

Figure 6.2 Clay pots for fermenting chicha, set deep into the ground

them by cords; these store all sorts of items. One sees carrying nets (*jerro*) with all sorts of things, for example, new *guacales* (drinking cups). The guacales (*pupa*) are mostly plain, only rarely with some decoration (through impressions made with the fingernails on the fresh guacal fruit). Frequently they are also made into sieves (*lhijílha*) by boring holes in them, as the Talamanca Indians also do. (See chapter 7, this volume.) During the preparation of chicha, cooked bananas are pushed through the sieve. The chicha itself is not fermented in wooden containers as among the Talamanca Indians but in very large clay pots (*chíu*) with inch-thick walls; these are made by the women. Most of these pots have a diameter and height of about 80 cm. They are set fairly deep into the ground, as shown in figure 6.2. The upper opening of the pots is covered by a peculiar round sieve (*chiqui*) made of basket-weave fiber that is also used for drying meat over the fire.

The only small cooking utensils I have seen are small pots for warming water. The rest are large clay cooking pots that must be rather hard to lift when they are hot. From time to time one sees bottle gourds (*quirrímun*). The large milling stones (*tumba*) of the Talamancas are unknown here. One does see smaller ones of the normal Middle American size, usually with three legs but at times without legs. Milling is done on them with round or oval manos. This just about takes care of the interior furnishings of the Guatuso palenque. Occasionally, there are two strong, smooth wooden poles stuck into the earth at a proper distance from each other, which serve to knot ropes into a hammock.

The most interesting aspect of a Guatuso palenque is that some burials are inside the house. They are perpendicular to the main direction of the house, as far as I could see. Normally these burials are surrounded by a balustrade of thin wooden poles so that nobody steps on them. I was told that the burials are not deep. The body, wrapped in bark (*mastate*) and clothed in new vestments, is placed in the grave, the bottom of which is covered by wooden poles and leaves. Bananas, cacao, and fire-making equipment are placed around the cadaver. Formerly fire-making consisted of rubbing together two pieces of a dried creeper (*carréjor*); now matches and easily burning wood are used. Then the body is covered with sticks and leaves, and earth is put over it to cover. This earth is not tamped down, so that the gases of disintegration can escape easily and at times fill the house. Even so, the Guatusos remain in their house, a most unhygienic and at the same time unpleasant stay. The Guatusos believe that the cadaver could do miracles and they therefore have a sort of ancestor cult with the grave. For them this burial is a holy place.

It is completely different if a person is bitten by a snake and dies as a result, because the Guatusos, similarly to the Q'eqchi' Indians, believe snakes to be servants of a god who uses them to punish mankind. The person who dies of snakebite is buried outside the house, his grave is not cared for, and his widow may not remarry and will not be touched again. The whole population of a palenque stays awake the entire night after such a death in order to defend themselves against a possible attack of the spirit; all formerly used guacales are thrown out and new ones put into use.

The weapons of the Guatusos consist of bows and arrows, although in recent times they have also acquired some rifles. Since they do not treat the guns with the necessary care, one can rather frequently find totally inoperable rifles among them. The arrows of the Guatusos correspond exactly to the fish arrows of the Talamanca Indians. An insert (50 cm or more in length) of round pejibaye wood that has been point-whittled on each end is placed into a 1.75-m-long tube. The bow is also made from pejibaye wood, has a flat crosscut, and is 125 to 140 cm long. The arrows serve for hunting as well as fishing. Fish are also caught with nets and most recently with fishing poles. Large game animals (wild boars, jaguars, tapirs) are caught by the Guatusos in deep pits that are wider at the bottom and whose openings are carefully covered by sticks and leaves. Birds are caught with slings.

For agricultural work the Guatusos use steel axes and machetes, as are used all over Middle America. A few years ago they still used two-sided, crudely worked flint axes; I secured only one single example after much effort. (I have sent it along with other items of the Guatusos to the Ethnographical Museum in Stuttgart.) To cut weeds, the Guatusos use machetes of pejibaye wood. These are about 1.5 m long, straight wooden sticks about 5 cm wide and 1.0 to 1.5 cm thick; they are pointed at the front end and given a sharp edge on one side. This sharp edge was obliterated on samples I was shown because they were no longer used as machetes but only as guidelines for sowing corn.

Before we left the first palenque, our guide took an arrow-tube out of a quiver, put a palm leaf into it, and bent it in a southeast direction as a sign of the direction taken. We found similar signs with bent leaves again later on our path near the footprints of a tapir.

After a short hike we arrived at the palenque of Nicolás, where I met the first Guatusos: weak and sickly looking people with surprisingly thin legs and fairly broad shoulders. Their mouth is large, their hair normally long and unkempt, occasionally cut half-short. The men have a very thin mustache and beard. I did not notice underarm hair on either men or women. Their clothing is quite varied; they wear all kinds of different pieces of European garments, just as they have been ac-

Figure 6.3
Guatuso Indians.
Photo by K.
Sapper

cidentally found. Bishop Thiel once met a Guatuso Indian who wore a tailcoat along with a breechcloth.

The original Indian attire for men consisted simply of a breechcloth (*jélenh*) made of bark material (*mastate*). The sample that I collected is a bark material strip about 3.6 m long and 28 cm wide. This strip is pulled between the legs, then wound around the hips with a rather long piece hanging down in front. Women's clothing consists of a piece of bark material wound around the hips and kept in place by tucking one corner into the front of the "skirt" (figure 6.3). The female garment (*quirrílenh*) I collected is a strip of bark material 1.48 m in length and 44 cm in width. The Guatusos originally did not wear hats (or sandals), although currently they are sometimes worn. Often one can find Guatusos with white or black strips wound around their heads. These hairbands consist mostly of very fine bark material (*cotí pal*),[2] while the ordinary bark material comes from the mastate or rubber trees. The outfits of the men also include a stick without a point. During fes-

tivities the more affluent Guatusos wear necklaces (*cólocóma*) of jaguar teeth. Men and women oil their bodies with cocoa butter, and during festivities they paint their oily body with red and yellow as well as black stripes on face, chest, and stomach. Women sometimes wear necklaces of false pearls.

The Guatusos rest by sitting on a low piece of wood, keeping their knees apart, and resting their elbows on their knees. Another posture is to rest with deeply bent knees, keeping their heels close together without touching, supporting an elbow on their knee, and holding their chin in their hand. This is the same attitude one can see on many stone sculptures of gods made by the old Güétaros (Huetars) in the highlands of Costa Rica.

The Guatusos are generally quite weak and suffer frequently from large abscesses, tuberculosis, or malaria. I saw just one child in the palenque of Nicolás and only a few in the following palenques. They hid the children from me, afraid I would take them away. This fear arose from the fact that earlier chicle collectors from Nicaragua robbed the Guatusos of their children and sold them in Nicaragua, where they are said to have received 50 pesos for each child. Since the government of Costa Rica established a frontier post in Río Frío, the intrusions of the chicle collectors have stopped. Shortly before my arrival, however, the Costa Rican authorities had taken two Guatuso children to San José for their education, and so I was regarded with suspicion and was kept as much as possible away from the children.

The children are said to be mostly male, so that the existing majority of males vis-à-vis females will increase. This predominance of males over females has resulted in polyandry becoming established among the Guatusos, although officially a woman is married to only one man.

Marriage occurs through purchase. The price is usually a certain quantity of cacao or a wild boar. There is no special marriage ceremony; the young husband moves into the palenque of his in-laws. A woman goes near water to give birth. As soon as the child is born, the cord is cut with a knife (formerly with a flint knife). After that mother and child are bathed and the child is oiled with cocoa butter reddened by an admixture of *achiote* (ground small red seeds of the annatto tree [*Bixa orellana*]). The child, colored red, is then brought into the house and the father stays in the hammock for about one month, guarding the child.

After leaving the palenque of Nicolás we soon came to the palenque of Pedro Jerez, where we found a large number of mildly drunk males and females having a big party. With loud calls of "lhaca," we were welcomed and offered chicha in large guacales, so that I could only defend myself with difficulty. A number of the women squatted in the middle of the palenque, chewing cooked manioc with full cheeks. When they had chewed it sufficiently they took the wads out of their mouths and made chicha after it had once more been milled. Chicha made of manioc is preferred by the Guatusos to the somewhat more appetizingly prepared chicha made from corn, bananas, or pejibaye.

According to Bishop Thiel, the Guatuso women also chew roasted cacao beans and then use the chewed cacao with hot water to make co-

coa, while they oil themselves with the cocoa butter. The main food of the Guatusos is bananas that are planted in large numbers on plantations (*chagüites*), as well as corn, manioc, and pejibaye fruit. Tortillas are as unknown here as among the Talamanca Indians; on the other hand, they make some other meals from corn, such as tamales (*púrrunh*) and *atole* (gruel made by boiling maize that has been pounded to a flour in water or milk). The Guatusos do not use salt; in its place, according to Thiel, they eat a clay-rich soil that contains aluminum.

Hunting and fishing provide some enrichment to the kitchen; even somewhat smelly meat is eaten. Of all wild animals only the deer is not hunted, because according to Thiel they believe that the souls of the deceased use the body of the deer as a residence if the souls do not move about in the dark of the forest all alone. So that these loose souls can get something to eat, the Guatusos from time to time put some cacao in guacales on their graves.

Nothing definite is known about the religious beliefs of the Guatusos. They recognize the sun (*toji*) as their god, the author of all goodness, and they assemble in front of its stone monument at a hidden place once a year to sacrifice chocolate. In addition they also recognize a bad spirit[3] (Thiel 1896:82). Nominally, the Guatusos have accepted Christianity, but in fact neither Catholic nor Protestant missionaries have achieved a real success. (A feeling of personal gratitude and loyalty connects them with Bishop Thiel, so that yearly a number of Guatusos go to San José to visit him and to receive presents of clothes and tools.)

To find out the will of the god(s), they use the well-known whizzing wood whose presence in all parts of the earth J.D.E. Schmeltz has proven in his excellent monograph (1896). The whizzing wood (*lhafára*) of the Guatusos is a piece of heavy sword-like wood, 30 to 35 cm long, 5 to 6 cm wide, and about 0.75 cm thick. Its front end is usually pointed but is sometimes cleanly cut; its other end is perforated. It is whirled through the air on a thin cord made from burillo bast. The main Indian who understands divining the will of the gods through the noise of the whizzing wood lives in

Figure 6.4
Guatuso melody
heard at night at
palenque
Margarita

palenque Sabára, located between the palenques of Nicolás and Pedro Jerez. There we saw several whizzing woods. Above a rather new, bad-smelling grave was a very peculiar little sack of tree rind material. When we opened it we found some red tail feathers of a *guacamaya* (macaw) and a wreath made of the red down feathers of the same bird. My guide explained that the wreath is placed on the head of the deceased laid out in state, and the tail feathers are put into his hands.

Toward evening we reached palenque Margarita (80 m) which consists of two huge houses next to one another, with thirty fireplaces. Each family usually has one fireplace; childless widowers also keep one. In front of the residences are two half-houses that contain only graves. In one of the residence houses we were given a place where we could hang up a hammock and spend the night. The hammock had barely been put up when an Indian lay down in it; as soon as that one got up, another did the same, so that only very late could I take possession of my own hammock.

The Guatusos are generally rather aggressive and can become a nuisance. Spoiled by the presents of the missionaries, they beg every stranger for a shirt or another article of clothing and if one gives them anything, they are even more persistent. When I had given quinine to a sick Indian, the entire company also wanted quinine, even though it does not taste good. The women are not much less aggressive than the men, and some shoved back my sleeves and caressed my arm with their hands while saying in their broken Spanish "bonito" (beautiful).

Finally it became quiet in the palenque; it might have been 8:30 at night. The people retired to their fireplaces; one of them sang a lengthy song before going to sleep, but I did not understand a word of its text. The melody started with some sounds in the "fifth" followed by a number of sounds in the "sixth" (sometimes large, sometimes small sixth). Then came the ending in a long-held tone in the fifth, which finally fast finished with a very short tone in "terz" or "third." Later on I heard other melodies, including the one in figure 6.4.

Of musical instruments I saw only a drum (*tali*), about 80 cm long and 20 cm in diameter, exactly as found among the Talamanca Indians, covered on only one side by the skin of an iguana. Unfortunately, I have seen none of the dances of the Guatusos. According to Thiel (1896:77) an Indian steps to a certain point, lifts the guacal filled with chicha to the height of his chest, and goes six or seven steps forward; then he stops and continues singing. He drinks his chicha and then hands the guacal to the next dancer. Frequently, three or four do this sort of dance together.

The following morning I went with my guide to the more distantly located palenques, Tojibar (145 m) and Cucaracha (65 m), where we received a friendly welcome. We were no longer bothered by begging, since these distant houses have been rather rarely visited by missionaries and other strangers. I did not have enough time to visit the most distant palenques of La Muerte and Grecia.

Halfway between Margarita and Tojibar is a large stone covered on all sides by bas reliefs. Even though those sculptures are not too well preserved, they show clearly the formerly higher culture of the presently rather run-down Guatusos. A snail-like ornament caught my eye, since I have never before seen this motif in sculptures of Middle America.

After arriving again at the Río Frío on the evening of the 28th of April, I traveled the following day in the company of Juan Paesano and three Guatusos in a large boat down the river. It was a beautiful and quiet trip, only made difficult and a bit dangerous by a number of sandbanks and rather frequent tree trunks that had fallen into the river. Since the sharks of Lake Nicaragua swim quite far upstream on the Río Frío, one is in danger if the boat capsizes. Despite this somewhat disagreeable thought, I enjoyed the lovely trip between the marvelous green walls of forest on each side, only rarely replaced by extended plains of reeds. Gradually we saw here old acquaintances from northern Middle America which are missing in most of Costa Rica, such as the lovely corozo palm, the prickly mach palm, the huge ceiba trees, the shady amate, and others. Numerous palms and leaf-trees of Costa Rica grow here as well. Some very pretty lianas of blue and white flowers hang from the trees right down to the top of the water. Every turn of the river provides new, surprising views of vegetation to the enchanted eye.

Shortly after the first curves of the river, we heard calls from the left bank and met three Costa Ricans who had become lost on their way from Cañas to Río Frío, so that they now stood at the edge of the river and could go no farther. Since our boat was rather large, we could accommodate them and continued our trip with the augmented crew. Fortunately, two of the guests were familiar with rowing and from time to time gave our poor Guatusos a chance to rest.

The longer I looked at those little people the more I became full of compassion for them, because they are truly good-natured human beings, even though very limited spiritually and, for that reason, also to a certain degree unreliable. To a large extent they have a feeble constitution, even at times approaching being crippled. One of our boat people could not walk properly and had a crooked spine. He was the best of the three Guatusos, since he showed the greatest intelligence and interest in his work. The other two had straight bodies, but were sickly and weak and completely without interest so that one had to call their attention to each obstruction in the river.

At every small stop one or another of the Guatusos bathed, and I was told that in other ways they also pay much attention to the cleanliness of their body. If they attend to all natural needs in the water, this custom may be quite comfortable and advantageous for the individual. For the tribal associates who live below on the same stream and get their drinking water from it, however, the practice is not particularly hygienic nor appetizing.

After having spent the night in the small settlement of Caño Negro, on the evening of 29 April we arrived at San Carlos where the American engineers of the Nicaragua Canal Commission extended the heartiest hospitality to me even though I was unknown to them. When I tried the following morning to look for my Guatusos, to give them some food for their return home and some messages for the commander of Río Frío, they had already disappeared.

Following them in my thoughts on their painful return trip I also thought of the entire unfortunate tribe, which will have died out shortly. Only forty years ago the Guatusos were feared as a warlike people and were able to turn back armed attacks by Nicaraguan chicle collectors. About 30 years ago the Nicaraguans formed a large force and, in a regular battle at the confluence of the Chincheritas brook, killed the caciques of the Guatusos. Guatuso resistance was broken and a time of misery followed when they were employed by these chicle collectors as slaves. At the same time they were robbed by them of food and children. These encroachments by the Nicaraguans came to an end only after the Costa Rican government, largely as a result of the reports of Bishop Thiel, finally placed a military post at Río Frío. Thiel himself had undertaken a trip into the territory of the Guatusos, where he was arrested by the Nicaraguans as a spy as he came down the Río Frío to San Carlos. Later trips endeared him to the Guatusos. Even if he did not succeed in civilizing them, he has nevertheless succeeded in improving their existence. His name is always honored when anyone speaks of the Guatusos.

NOTES
1. We have been unable to determine the location of "Calderas."
2. Sapper used *cucánhíya* and *cotí pal* as if they were synonyms. They are not. See glossary.
3. Sapper provided "*oronco* or *macháro*" as the Guatuso words for "a bad spirit"; however, "Oronhcaf" is the proper name for the chief of the devils of the sky and *macháro* is simply a generic term for evil spirit.

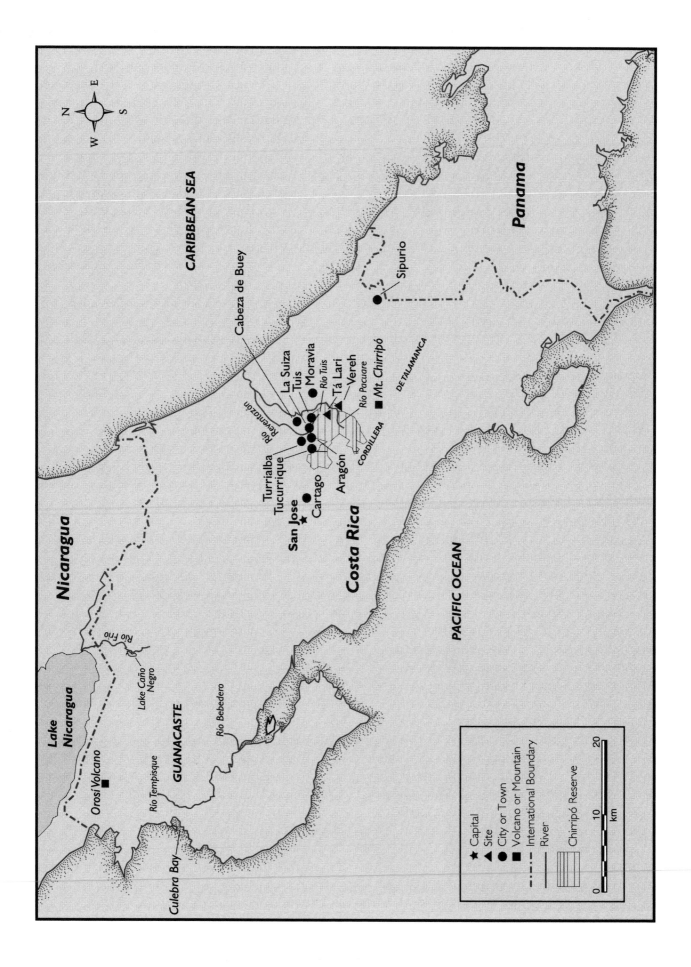

CHAPTER 7

A Visit with the Chirripó and Talamanca Indians

Karl Sapper

Originally published as
"Ein Besuch bei den Chirripó- und Talamanca-Indianern von Costarica"
Globus 77(1900):1-8
Braunschweig: Druck und Verlag von Friedrich Vieweg und Sohn

COMMENTARY

When I first read this article I had returned from an extended stay in Costa Rica. After sixteen months in Guanacaste, scrambling around Culebra Bay or climbing about a petroglyph field on Orosí volcano, I took an additional two trips, one to the Reserva Indigena Chirripó (Chirripó Indian Reserve), the other to Mount Chirripó. Each journey was physically excruciating in its own way because of conditions described by Sapper: heat and/or cold, pelting rain or intense sun, steep mountains, and high altitude. Mine were thrilling adventures, and as I read Sapper's journey through Talamanca, I relived my own travels along similar, and in some parts the same, roads. I experienced the heat and humidity, the shortness of breath, and the smells.

Beginning in San José we went to Cartago and then Turrialba, passing through the small towns of La Suiza and Tuis—about three hours by car. Outside Tuis, we parked the car in a villager's front yard and cut down the mountain across a *quebrada* (dry stream channel) to a logging road that leads to the south. We followed this road uphill for approximately two hours until we arrived at a small, well-worn path that led downhill into the Reserva Indigena Chirripó and then the village of Vereh after about another two hours. What had taken Sapper three days to reach by train and foot in 1899 had taken less than seven hours in 1994.

When Sapper reports climbing to 970 m (Gracias a Dios) I wondered if he was referring to a village or the mountain peak of that name or was expressing his anguish at traveling at such high altitude. Having walked 1000 m up to Mount Chirripó, I'm partial to the latter interpretation. Sapper's trip took him farther and higher into Talamanca; I spent three days camped along Río Pacuare where I met Aníbal Reyes, a Cabécar medicine shaman.

A colleague accompanying me, an Indian botanist, suggested I not ask the shaman any direct questions. Any knowledge would have to come from the shaman, as I had no right to things that were not my business. Pondering this limitation, I was introduced to Aníbal as an archaeologist. Aníbal asked me the pointed question many archaeologists fear, "How many people like me have you talked to?" "Very few," I admitted, "and you are my first shaman."

He showed me the inside of the *palenque* (dwelling built of posts) his people had just built (see fig. 7.1). Roomy and dark, it was their hospital, with a fire in the center, hammocks, low wooden benches, some cots for the infirm, and many things tucked along the walls. For the Bribris and Cabécar, the structure of the conical house (*u-suré, jutsini*), or *templo cosmico*, represents their cosmic view; it was created, organized, and given to them by the creator Sibú at the time of creation, its ritual construction and symbols the domain of the *Awa'/Jawa'* (medical specialist) (González and González 1989:14).

As a Cabécar shaman, Aníbal treats his own villagers and also travels over the mountains to more remote areas giving aid to the sick. Many plants important to his cures and ceremonies are getting harder to find and grow only far from his home. Aníbal's dream is to have a garden next to the hospital where all his medicinal plants can grow and be available when he needs them.

The next morning Aníbal took me to Tá Lari, an archaeological site nearby. He remembered the names of the Costa Rican archaeologists who worked there. Returning to the village, he asked if I would take some pictures of him. He disappeared for a while, then reappeared, having donned a white long-sleeved shirt. Eagle feathers were held on his forehead by a leather strap. In his right hand he clutched his "power stick" (what Sapper calls walking stick, see fig. 7.8), and his left hand held his "medicine stick" (*uru'*). A pouch containing "special things" and a loupe hung around his neck. I took his picture standing in front of his hospital palenque. He let me take close-ups of his medicine stick and explained the images he had drawn on it.

Aníbal Reyes

He then changed his white shirt for one with a Hawaiian print that he often wears. It was time for a healing ceremony to begin and he invited me to observe and take pictures. His patients, two young girls with intestinal disorders, lay on mats on the floor. It was very dark. By firelight (from across the room) I watched a ceremony that involved waving feathers and special plants over the bodies. The shaman then killed a chicken, extracted its heart, and rubbed it over each girl's stomach and chest. The younger child cried and the ceremony ended quickly. Nearly everyone was happy or at least relieved, except me. I could hardly see, and I knew the photos would be very poor. A bowl of pejibaye appeared. I helped peel their skins.

Early the following and final morning, Aníbal offered me, upon arrival at the palenque, *chicha* (corn beer). We drank it for a couple of hours while I took many pictures of him and his family, the hospital, and so on. He invited me to return and document more of his curing ceremonies. I felt honored to have met him, to have been invited into his hospital, and to have observed his ceremonies.

Looking up from my computer to the wall covered with photographs of that trip, I see Aníbal in dress shirt, feathered headdress, pouch, loupe, power stick, and medicine stick; Aníbal firing a bow and arrow made of pejibaye wood; Aníbal with a close-up of the medicine stick with figures he tells me represent healing spirits, medicinal plants, and the illnesses he hopes to cure. One figure, an anthropomorph with feathered headdress and upraised arms, stands out—a figure many call a shaman, though to Aníbal it is a spirit. Finally, there is a group portrait taken in front of the hospital palenque. I recall how I felt at that time, sweating from the heat and humidity or perhaps from the chicha at seven o'clock in the morning. I am the tallest in the photo. There I stand, holding the chicha bottle, Aníbal to my left wearing a yellow soccer shirt, his loupe and medicine pouch around his neck, with the chicha cup in his hand. A small child peers between us. Aníbal's son and two grandsons stand to my right.

Aníbal invited me to return to the palenque. He especially wanted me to make a video recording of his healing ceremonies. I sit here waiting to return. I gave him a Museo Nacional T-shirt that pictures an upside-down anthropomorph with feathered headdress who appears to be in a trance or perhaps in flight, a motif found on a petroglyph from the Orosí volcano. He gave me memories I'll cherish forever.

—Ellen T. Hardy

A Visit with the Chirripó and Talamanca Indians

After a month-long visit in the central highlands of Costa Rica with its dense population, its highly developed agriculture, and the relatively advanced civilization of its inhabitants, I was eager to explore the less populated south of the country with its tremendous mountains and virgin forests and its Indian inhabitants, who so far have been scarcely touched by the influence of European civilization. Even so, the rain-forest highlands had deeply impressed me with the beauty of their landscape and magnificent volcanoes.

It was not easy for me to determine a route that would allow me a general view of the types of mountains and forests but would also allow me to record the peculiarities of the original inhabitants in their out-of-the-way settlements, thus increasing the present knowledge of Costa Rica. While the largest part of this area had been unknown, my honored friend Professor H. Pittier has recently traveled there extensively and investigated it thoroughly (Pittier 1898). Pittier advised me to take the road from Turrialba (Angostura Province) to Talamanca, a path that at one time was much traveled, now almost totally abandoned but shown schematically on the map of Costa Rica by Friederichsen (1876).

This road was traveled by the courageous and dedicated Bishop of Costa Rica, Dr. Bernhard Thiel, on a mission journey during which he was exposed to great hardships as well as dangers on account of the rainy season (December 1889 to January 1890). Since Dr. Thiel did not make any road surveys, the report of his journey (1896:36–51) throws little light on the topographic conditions of that region, and a renewed walk along that road appeared worthwhile.

I left San José de Costa Rica on 18 March 1899 in the company of my porter, Sebastián Ical, who had come with me from Guatemala, and we took the train via Cartago to the Tucurrique station. This station is separated by the deep canyon of the Río Reventazón from the Indian village of the same name, beautifully located on a mountain road. From there we went on foot along the railroad bed to the Turrialba station to complete a previous hike along the railroad bed to La Junta and to investigate the geology of this part of the line.

After provisioning ourselves in Turrialba with sufficient food for the following day's journey, I started the trip to Talamanca from the coffee and sugar plantation Aragón (660 m altitude). A well-maintained cart road leads into the deep valley of the Río Reventazón whose foamy and noisy waters one crosses on a good bridge (530 m). The road rises to the scattered houses of Angostura Province (580 m altitude) and leads from there into the beautiful valley of the Río Tuis. There, a number of promising coffee plantations have sprung up since the opening of the railroad, mostly owned by British, American, or Swiss people. I spent the night at the coffee plantation La Suiza, located near the settlement of Tuis

Bribri Glossary

Native word	Spelling in original	Spanish	English
ali'	arí	yuca	Manioc (*Manihot utilissima* or *M. esculenta*)
Awa'		médico aborigen	Medical specialist
datsi'	datzí		Cloth
diko'	dikó	pejibaye	Pejibaye palm
dipa'	dipá	chile	Chile pepper (*Capsicum annuum*)
Sibu'			Creator of the world
uru'			Wood or balsa trunk painted by the Awa' and used in therapeutic curing rituals.
u-suré		casa conica	Conical house

Cabécar Glossary

Native word	Spelling in original	Spanish	English
diká	diká	pejibaye	Pejibaye palm (*Guilielma utilis* Oerd. or *Bactris gasipaes*)
datsí			Cloth
Jawa'		médico aborigen	Medical specialist
jutsiní		casa conica	Conical house
Sibu'			Creator of the world
uru'			Wood or balsa trunk painted by the Jawa' and used in therapeutic curing rituals.

(700 m altitude) where I was able to obtain a guide for the first part of my journey up to the Indian settlements of Moravia and El Arenal.

We had barely reached the settlement of Tuis when we left the cart road and followed a narrow, but much used, footpath. The path led us immediately into dense virgin forest that covers the entire Atlantic declivity of the large Costa Rican mountain chain. Because of the extraordinarily low population density of this area there are only a few places where the forest has been cut and is now replaced by meadows. This virgin forest reminded me in its overall character of the similar rain forests of Guatemala, Honduras, or Nicaragua, with its many strong deciduous trees; its exuberant climbers and its luxuriant low-growing plants; its epiphytes, palm trees, and ferns. It made a strange impression on me, however; the plant species are mostly different from those of my adoptive home in Guatemala, since the area of South American flora starts in Costa Rica.

Our path was here and there quite tiring on account of the occasional tremendously steep climbs, but since I had just spent a long time wandering in the open sun-drenched area of Guanacaste and Nicoya and in the dusty highways of the highlands, I was delighted to be able to walk again in the shadows of the forest. My Indian companion also felt himself in his element, as the forest reminded him of his home in the Alta Verapaz. Thus we happily plowed along our path over the foothills of the great central mountain chain, which here, at first, does not reach high elevations. We climbed to 970 m ("Gracias a Dios"), descended to the Cabeza del Buey brook (590 m altitude), climbed up again to 730 m, and finally descended to the Río Pacuare (490 m altitude), which we waded without difficulty. On the other side we found a well-preserved, sufficiently large protective roof, so we started our bivouac early and enjoyed the quiet with all the contemplative comfort which in good weather is customary in camps in silent virgin forests. A serpent made its way between me and my companion during our meal, temporarily disturbing our peace but was quickly overtaken by its fate.

Continuing our trip on 21 March, we first had to cross the Río San Rafael, a tributary of the Pacuare. With larger rivers my habit is to disrobe and wade through by myself; with smaller ones my porter carries me across on his back. In this case our guide offered to carry me across the little river and I accepted to save the short delay when the porter first crosses with his load and then must return to carry me. As I was about to swing up onto the back of our guide I suddenly felt a strong pain on my right side. Our guide had forgotten to remove his machete which was strapped to his back. As I collided with its handle I injured a rib on my right side, which caused me much pain during the next three weeks and considerably restricted my mobility. Nevertheless we continued our travel and ascended a steep grade on a narrow path through a delightful forest, with charming small palm trees among the thicket of trees, lianas, and low-growing shrubs. In slow ascent one can observe that the palm trees become more sparse and tree ferns take their place.

At El Surtubal (980 m altitude) a longish stone can be seen (about 120 cm long, 25 cm thick, and 21 cm wide) on which some crude figures have been carved. According to my guide the Chirripó Indians call this stone "Cristóbal" and are accustomed to play with it as they pass it, taking it on their shoulders and then putting it down. I concluded that this stone must have been deliberately dragged to this place, because on the entire grade we found no undecomposed, solid stone.

After El Surtubal the ascent is less steep, and after passing a height of 1180 m one arrives at a somewhat marshy plateau on which the first houses of the Chirripó Indians are located, here called Moravia and El Arenal (1100 m). The latter is the residence of the Justice of the Peace, Nicolás Moya, to whom I was to present my letters of recommendation to engage a guide for the continuation of the trip. Since the Señor Justice of the Peace could neither read nor write and could not even understand Spanish completely, it was the habit of travelers to show him any kind of piece of paper to engage a guide or other help. When we arrived in El Arenal, Moya was absent, as he went for some days to Tuis as many Chirripó Indians now do in order to find work at one of the plantations and earn some money. At the same time he also tried to sell chickens or hogs and bring home in trade salt, cotton cloth, powder, and lead. Even though the Chirripó Indians still use bow and arrows, they are beginning to use guns, which are preferable for hunting. Since powder and lead shot are relatively expensive, one occasionally comes across Indians who carry a bow and a bundle of arrows along with their gun.

We had arrived at noon at El Arenal, and so we had time to inspect in detail the habitation, its furniture, and clothing and weapons of the Chirripó Indians, as well as to observe some of their habits. For simplicity, I am anticipating my later observations and intersperse them here in an attempt to give a sketch of the Indians' present

Figure 7.1 Oval palenque of the Talamanca Indians

cultural level. Some of the photographs from the San José de Costa Rica Gallery of Art serve as additional evidence. The photos were taken in Talamanca, but the Chirripó Indians are ethnologically the same as the Bribri Indians who live in Talamanca, and speak a similar language. The illustrations are therefore quite adequate.

The typical residence of the Chirripó and Talamanca Indians (figure 7.1) is a round hut of considerable size (between 12 and 20 m in diameter at ground level) with a steeply built roof (40° to 45°) that reaches to the ground (figure 7.2a). One low entrance, or two opposite each other, frequently protected by a little flat roof, leads to the interior. The entrances are the only sources of light, since windows and other openings are lacking. As a result, semi-darkness permeates the interior during the entire day. The roof (figure 7.2a, b) rests on eight fairly irregularly set posts in an eight-cornered pattern, and the posts are connected by crossbeams. Strong poles rest on these crossbeams, and the palm-frond roof is fastened to them. The poles meet at the top of the roof and are pulled together to a short, often vaulted ridge, also cov-

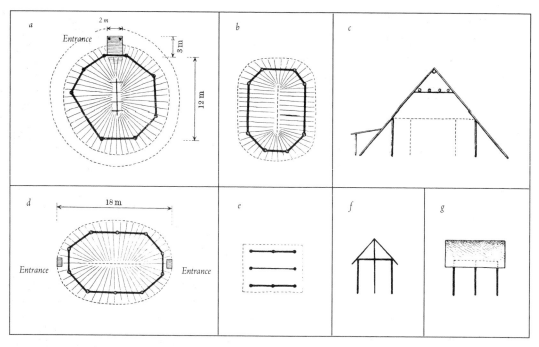

Figure 7.2
Examples of
palenques: a, El
Arenal; b,
Moravia; c,
section of El
Arenal palenque;
d, Xiquiari; e–g,
plan, section, and
side view of
simple structure at
Xiquiari

ered with palm leaves. At the three-quarter height of the building some horizontal round crossbeams are attached in the interior to increase its sturdiness (figure 7.2c).

The floor consists of tamped earth; at times the entrance is protected against mud by a bridge of perpendicularly laid round wooden poles. Animals are kept out of the house either by crossed wooden rails at the entrance(s) or by a fence surrounding the entire house.

Frequently the palenques are elongated, as at Xiquiari (figure 7.2d), and are then apparently based on ten posts, probably a recent development. In these cases the roofs of such houses do not reach down to the ground. Instead, the roof ends at the height of a man, and a wall of upright wooden stakes is constructed some feet from the base pillars. The palenques are meant for several families, each having their own hearth. Single families build only open huts for themselves, without walls but with a simple two-sided roof (figure 7.2e, f, g). All the inhabitants of a hamlet customarily help in the construction of a residence. Only two men are needed to repair a roof, one working inside and the other outside the hut.

In the interior of the palenque the location of the fireplaces, as well as the sleeping accommodations, are notable. For sleeping, a woven mat of bark materials covers bamboo staves. Hammocks are generally made of firm materials, only rarely of woven or knotted ropes, and are used only for resting, not for sleeping. Often a rope, suspended from the roof beams, holds some beautiful bird skins or feathers, and frequently long, colorful bird feathers are stuck into the roof. Several strong ropes hold a platform of tied sticks on which food and other items are kept out of the reach of ants. Some ropes are also available for hanging clothes or bananas. Horizontal sticks stuck into the wall next to the bed hold bows, arrows, and blowpipes.

Frequently, peculiar vessels made of loose basketry held together at the upper end by a strong hoop (*jabas* in Spanish) are attached to posts. Also, low stools on four legs and low wooden benches are said to be offered to visitors to sleep on. Besides ceramic pots there is also enameled iron cookware. *Tecomates* (bottle gourds) and wooden drinking bowls (*guacales* or *jícaras*) are used here as well as all over Middle America. Some of the gourds have holes for use as sieves in the preparation of chicha. Chicha is made of corn, bananas, and manioc. This mildly intoxicating, fermented drink is brewed in large wooden containers. It is consumed daily by the Indians in large quantities, as they have coffee only rarely.

The main food staple of the Chirripó and Talamanca Indians is the *plátano*, the large plaintains known by that name in Middle America

*Figure 7.3
Talamanca
women milling on
tumbas*

*Figure 7.4
Talamanca man
fishing*

Figure 7.5 River scene in Talamanca

Figure 7.6 Talamanca women carrying loads

and grown in large plantations. Before their starch content has had a chance to change into sugar, they are taken out of their green outer skins and either roasted or cooked in water. They can also be cut into small pieces, cooked in water until soft, then squeezed by hand in cold water and consumed as a pulpy drink. Not much corn is grown, and most of that is used in making chicha. The metates used in Middle America, on which the Indian women mill the softened corn using an elongated mano, are unknown here. Instead, the cooked corn is crushed and milled by using a large, round stone on top of a large flat one or on a wooden board; the round stone is moved back and forth and its weight does the job (figure 7.3). The ladinos call this flat kind of milling stone *la tumba*.

In Xiquiari I once saw a small metate with a trough-like indentation, which would be used similarly to a mortar. The tumbas are generally not kept in the house but on the bank of a neighboring brook. Tortillas, the corn cakes used all over Middle America, were unknown to the Indians of Costa Rica until a short time ago and so far have not become widely used.

Other foods worth mentioning besides bananas and corn are manioc (*ali'* in Bribri, *Manihot utilissima*) and the fruit of the pejibaye palm trees (*diká* in Cabécar, *diko'* in Bribri, *Guilielma utilis* Oerd.).[1] Red pepper or chile (*dipa'* in Bribri, *Capsicum annuum*) is used as spice. Hunting and fishing contribute their part in providing food for these Indians. Guns are used for hunting rather frequently by the Chirripó Indians, while the Talamanca Indians use them almost exclusively. Blowguns are used to hunt small birds, bow and arrows for other animals. Bows are whittled from the wood of the pejibaye palm and have tapered ends; they are about 1.5 m long and straight, unless under tension. A few arrows intended for large animals have steel points; the rest consist of two pieces: a light tube and a heavy insert made from the pejibaye wood. The points of most arrows are three cornered; at times, they have a round end with two or three rows of hooks attached. Since the insert has to be sharpened frequently with the bushknife, its length is always changing.

For various reasons, several Indians usually go

Figure 7.7 Indian women carrying children

Figure 7.8 Antonio Saldaña, king of Talamanca

Figure 7.9
William Gabb
and two other
Talamanca
men in their
best clothes

hunting together; for example, a large animal such as a tapir could not be transported home by a single person. They also use dogs for hunting; these, for instance, will chase a jaguar up a tree where it can be killed by an arrow with a metal point. If necessary, a man will climb a neighboring tree to get close enough to the jaguar to be sure to hit him.

They fish with arrows (figure 7.4). These consist of a very long tube (up to 1.75 m) into which the approximately 0.5 m long, round, well-pointed pejibaye palm insert is placed. If a fish is only wounded, it is followed until it tires and surfaces at one of the quiet water pools.

The Indians usually keep pigs and domestic fowl, and the richer ones engage in animal husbandry. By the sale of surplus animals, they acquire the money to purchase cotton material and other things that they cannot make. In Talamanca they also earn a good deal through transportation of freight in their flat boats (*pitpantes*); in quiet water the movement is provided by loose oars that are almost the same as those of the *canaletes* (dugout canoes) of the Middle American Caribs. In shallow water the boats are moved with long poles that also serve to diminish the movement in rapids (figure 7.5).

The Indians of Costa Rica carry loads in nets with the help of a band across the forehead (figure 7.6); frequently, a second band across the chest is also used to ease the load. Women, as well as men, carry loads; from time to time, one can see a man carrying only a bow and arrows or a hunting rifle and his hunting bag, while the woman following him carries the entire burden. Children are carried by the women on their backs, held in place by a broad scarf wrapped around the chest (figure 7.7).

Originally, the clothing of the Chirripó and Talamanca Indians consisted of a loincloth for men and a broad strip of bark material of the mastate tree for women. The bark of this tree is cooked, carefully peeled, and worked over a wooden pallet with a chamfered wooden tool. Then it is submerged in water, so that the bark juices, which would otherwise make the material prone to break, can escape. After that it is dried in the sun. The mastate cloth (*datsi'* in Bribri; *datsí* in Cabécar) is then fairly soft and pliable.

Currently, mastate is rarely used for clothing, but it is the common material for bedcovers. The dress for men or women resembles more and more that of the Europeans (figure 7.8). For this they use cotton fabrics. They do not know how to weave cotton, even though one sees a few cotton plants here and there. Most of the men wear their hair half long, and the mop of it almost looks like a cap, if the hair at the neck is shaved fairly far up. Originally, the Indians did not wear hats. The women wear their hair loose or loosely tied; frequently however, they make braids after the European custom. During fiestas the men wear their feather ornaments, which sometimes can be seen on a hook in their huts. A long stick completes their dress (figure 7.9).

Very little is known about the community and state government. The Bribri Indians still have a king, don Antonio Saldaña,[2] whose residence is in Túnsula near Sipurio; since they gladly follow his orders, the authorities in Talamanca rule by his mediation. Don Rafael Iglesias, the current president of Costa Rica, has made the king a sergeant and arranged for him to receive a salary of $40 a month. I do not know whether the Chirripó Indians also have a special political leader.

Pittier (1898) has reported extensively about a number of customs and habits of the Bribri Indians; here, I refer to his descriptions. The majority of the Indians have ostensibly taken on Christianity; whether they truly believe in it, however, and what the faith of their fathers was, I do not know.

I understand that the dead are placed on some

Figure 7.10 Snail flute melody of Chirripó Indians with typical ending

kind of rack not far from their residence to rot; afterward their bones are smoked over the fire in the house and finally buried in a sort of cemetery, the location of which is kept secret. One of these cemeteries is said to be in a cave in the Chirripó valley, while five others are located in Talamanca. The burial is accompanied by great drinking feasts during which the Indians, lined up in rows, sing certain songs while they beat drums covered by iguana skins. I cannot report the content of these songs as they are kept secret.

Apart from these drums I only became acquainted with a sort of snail flute that has a small number of very good sounds. It is made from the shell of a sea snail of about 6 cm in diameter with a hole drilled into the side; by blowing into the orifice, as into a flute, one can produce a few notes. The only player I heard achieved three sounds in a minor key; his short melodies with their sustained sounds and their nice harmony made a very agreeable impression upon me.

Since admittedly a certain modest artistic musical value was noticeable, I was interested in hearing larger productions, but unfortunately my hopes were not fulfilled. I can therefore give only a few short examples, whose ending cadences at times reminded me of the usual ending formulas of recitatives. These produced many memories for me, as they happily accompanied me during my further lonely wanderings in the rain forest. Figure 7.10 shows an example of the snail flute melody of the Chirripó Indians, typical of the ending of such melodies.

Furthermore, I was impressed by the chanting manner of speech of the Chirripó Indians. One of them, an old woman and the wife of the Justice of the Peace of El Arenal, would start her conversation at a high pitch and would end it almost an octave lower, while holding the same monotone for some time in between. The sons of the Justice of the Peace also spoke in a chanting manner but not to the same extent as their mother.

NOTES

1. *Manihot utilissima* used by Sapper is synonymous with *M. esculenta. Guilielma utilis* Oerd. used by Sapper is synonymous with *Bactris gasipaes.*

2. Sapper indicates "king" (*konig*) as opposed to *cacique*, the Taino word for head of household and a term used by the Spanish for chief. After warring for many years, the Cabécars and other Talamancan groups fell under the political rule of the Bribris, with one family holding the rights for hereditary chieftainship; the Cabécars held intellectual and religious supremacy insofar as their tribe maintained hereditary control of the religious leader *Usekara*, while the ordinary priests, also hereditary, belonged to the Bribris (Gabb 1876:488-489). Antonio Saldaña (figure 7.8) held the title "rey de Talamanca"; note his kingly symbols, including eagle feather headdress, collar of six large gold eagles, and walking or power stick. He died on 3 January 1910 after possibly having been poisoned (Stone 1961:208). More recent studies have increased our knowledge of Talamancan Indian cultures (Stone 1961, 1962, 1966; Bozzoli de Wille 1975, 1979).

KARL SAPPER

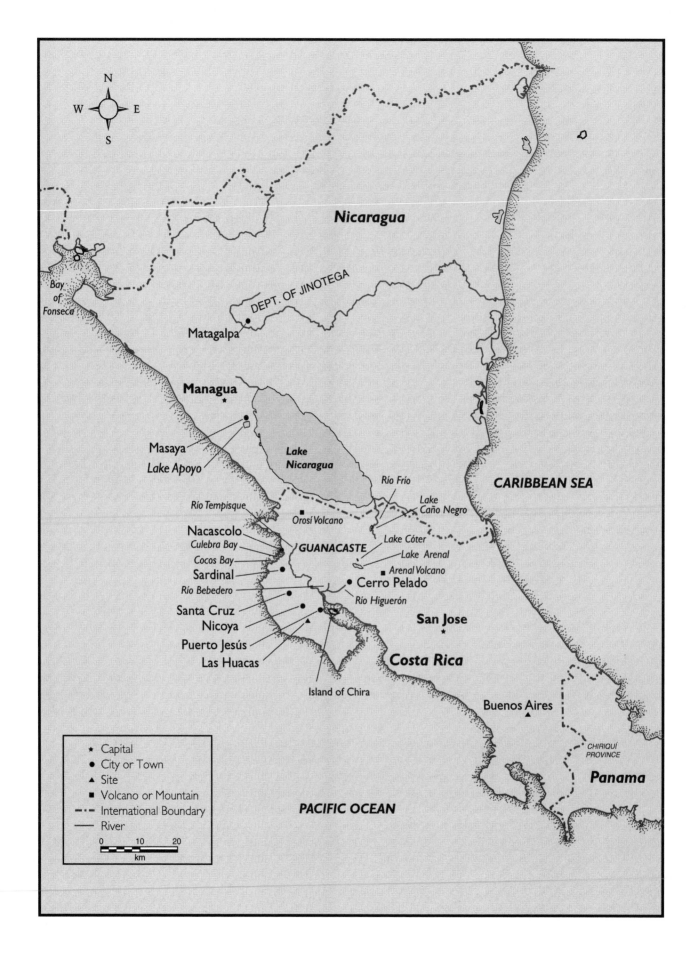

Nicaragua

Bay of Fonseca

DEPT. OF JINOTEGA

Matagalpa

Managua ★

Masaya

Lake Apoyo

Lake Nicaragua

Río Frío

CARIBBEAN SEA

Lake Caño Negro

Río Tempisque

Orosí Volcano

Nacascolo

Culebra Bay

GUANACASTE

Lake Cóter

Lake Arenal

Cocos Bay

Sardinal

Arenal Volcano

Río Bebedero

● **Cerro Pelado**

Río Higuerón

Santa Cruz

Nicoya

Puerto Jesús

San Jose ★

Las Huacas

Costa Rica

Island of Chira

Buenos Aires ▲

CHIRIQUÍ PROVINCE

Panama

★ Capital
● City or Town
▲ Site
■ Volcano or Mountain
–·– International Boundary
— River

0 10 20
km

PACIFIC OCEAN

CHAPTER 8

Huacas of the Nicoya Peninsula

Karl Sapper

Originally published as
"Huacas der Halb-Insel Nicoya"
Zeitschrift für Ethnologie 31(1899):622–632
Berlin: Museum für Völkerkunde

COMMENTARY

Sapper's assessment of Las Huacas as an archaeologically rich site that would provide archaeological data for many years has certainly proved accurate. Las Huacas cemetery continues as the standard to which all Greater Nicoya mortuary data are compared, remaining the pinnacle in size and complexity. Its archaeological collections continue to be analyzed and reanalyzed today. The Las Huacas collection acquired by Hartman remains the largest contextually documented pre-Columbian jade and greenstone collection from Costa Rica (Lange 1988:78). Stylistic analysis of this collection demonstrated some iconographic associations with South America and provided site dates of approximately AD 180 to 525 (Fonseca and Scaglion 1978:284). Sapper described ongoing excavations in the cemetery at Las Huacas in 1899 and noted undisturbed areas as well, contrasting with the ensuing pockmarked, moonscaped terrain.

I was fortunate to participate in projects where the first decorated Guanacaste metates were scientifically excavated from two different cemeteries at Nacascolo, Culebra Bay, in 1980 (Lawrence and Hardy 1982; Hardy 1992). Similar to those Sapper details from Las Huacas (fig. 8.2), both have animal heads and are decorated on the feet and upper and lower surfaces in geometric pattern, although subsequent mano use abraded the majority of the designs.

Notwithstanding this article's title, it contains more than just descriptions of tomb construction and burial content. Sapper provides data and analyses of other archaeological classes, including architecture, roads, ceramics, and metallurgy. He then takes us to Nicaraguan rock art and statuary. He was one of the first to make specific observations about ancient Costa Rican architecture, noting the meagerness of Guanacaste expressions in comparison to the impressive achievements of the Maya and Mexican areas.

Sapper's impressive insight about the introduction of metallurgy into Guanacaste has subsequently been borne out by archaeological research. Gold metallurgy, produced by gold leaf and casting by the lost-wax casting (cire-perdue) processes (the "gold-wire" artifacts of Lower Central America), spread gradually from south to north dating approximately 2000 to 1500 BC in Peru and being introduced into Mexico from AD 700 to 900 (Bray 1981:153). Gold working arrived in Greater Nicoya around AD 700 (Lange 1988:9). Noting the paucity of gold objects found in Nicoya in comparison to those of Costa Rica's other regions, Sapper posits their importation. Decades later, Day (1988:211) argues that gold was not intended for mortuary rites in Greater Nicoya but was a trade or tributary item, suggesting that elites received gold and passed it on to trade partners in Nicaragua as part of an extensive exchange system linking Costa Rica to the southern Mexican highlands, and specifically linking the Tempisque drainage with Nicaragua. Very few gold objects have Guanacaste provenience, and fewer have been recovered from archaeological contexts. In 1994 during salvage excavations at Finca Linares to allow construction of the grand entrance into Culebra Bay's tourist development (Proyecto Turístico Bahía Papagayo), a gold plate and a gold pendant were recovered from mortuary contexts. The pendant had been worn around the neck of the deceased individual, falling on top of the face during burial. A ceramic bowl, Galo Polychrome (ca. AD 500–800), was placed over the face. Finca Linares is located a few hundred meters south of the Río Tempisque.

Sapper recognized stylistic differences in architecture and rock art. He noted different petroglyph styles in southern and northern Nicaragua, roughly corresponding to what archaeologists would later define as part of the Greater Nicoya Archaeological Subarea (Norweb 1964) or outside its northeastern boundary. His descriptions and drawings of rock art from Santa Clara, Nicaragua, provide one of the earliest published renditions of petroglyph designs (fig. 8.7).

–Ellen T. Hardy

Huacas of the Nicoya Peninsula

The Nicoya peninsula of the Republic of Costa Rica is presently little known, yet belongs to the most fruitful archaeological region of all Central America. This is attested to by many finds from this area in the National Museum in the capital, San José. They bear witness to a vanished, fairly high culture that differed markedly from that of the Aztecs and from that of the Huetars who lived in the highlands of Costa Rica.

Most of the archaeological objects from Nicoya were found among the numerous middens and tombs of the ancient Indian settlements called *huacas* or *guacas* (funeral mounds) that are distributed over the entire peninsula. These huacas are said to be quite numerous, but I never got to see any on my journey from Cocos Bay and Sardinal to Santa Cruz, Nicoya, and Puerto Jesús. It was therefore necessary that I make a side trip from La Colonia to the last human habitation in the interior of the peninsula, which is called Las Huacas after the large number of remains of ancient Indian settlements. The owner of this solitary settlement, Antonio Carrillo,[1] is a simple but very hospitable man who received me cordially and became my willing guide during my short stay at his house. This gave me the opportunity to study a few huacas in some detail.

While the culture of the original inhabitants of Nicoya ranks considerably below that of the neighboring colonies of the Aztecs, it is much higher than the rest of the Indian tribes in Costa Rica and had in fact reached a fairly advanced stage. Thus I was disappointed when I considered their poor buildings. While architecture had reached a somewhat praiseworthy florescence among the Indian people of Mexico and northern Central America, it seems to have remained in its first beginnings in southern Middle America.

The huacas are very simple constructions with stone walls; they are usually arranged to form partially or completely enclosed level courtyards. According to my observations, single mounds never occur in the center, as is frequently the case in northern Middle America. The stone walls are low, not very broad, and constructed with plain river cobbles. According to Antonio Carrillo, occasionally the four corners of a simple court-huaca are formed by large, worked limestone blocks. In fact, at one spot he showed me two such isolated blocks of limestone that must have been carried a long way, since their nearest source is approximately 3 km distant.

Although the stone walls are generally very low, one does occasionally encounter clear steps, as for instance at the west wall of Huaca del Sitio de los Mayorgas (figure 8.1b) at the point where the incomplete diagonal cross wall would have intersected that west wall.

A remarkable enlargement and broadening of a wall is also visible at the northeast corner of the

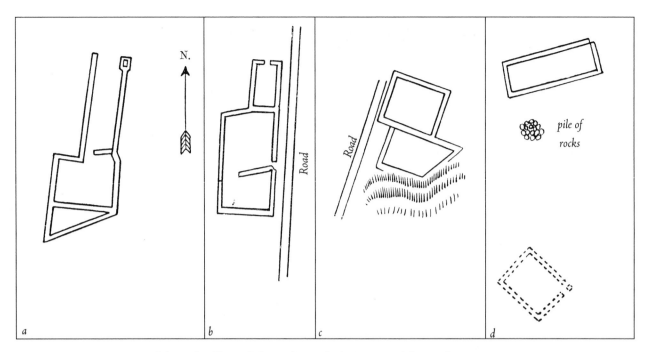

Figure 8.1 Plans of huacas: a, Huaca del Frijolar; b, Huaca del Sitio de los Mayorgas; c, Huaca de los Cañafistoles; d, Huaca de Esterones. Scale 1:1050

Huaca del Frijolar (fig. 8.1a), located near the residence of Sr. Carrillo. However, that specific part of the wall is so poorly preserved that nothing about the structural composition of the huaca could be determined. Pyramidal stepped platforms were apparently unknown here, although they were in general use in northern Middle America.

Where walls are built against a hill, as at the Huaca de los Cañafistoles (figure 8.1c), they were only half-built or indicated. These walls were between 1 and 2 m wide. In the case of the southern courtyard of the Huaca de Esterones (figure 8.1d), the stone walls are not standing but are only indicated by a row of stones; perhaps a heap of loose stones in the vicinity was meant to furnish the material for the residential building. In this case one can see clearly that the walls were constructed of dry masonry rather than of earth with stone coverings.

Often the stone walls clearly show an opening into the courtyard. In the case of the two courts of the Huaca de Esterones (figure 8.1d), this entrance is on the north side. The walls are generally connected at right angles, but walls at other angles are not rare. Three of the huacas I investigated were oriented approximately towards the cardinal directions, but Huaca de Esterones was not. In any event, for any single huaca a standard orientation was always maintained.

The roads are more important constructions than the huacas. They are still very clearly recognizable, especially in their fairly wide sunken beds and their straight alignments, which may extend for considerable distances. In some places, however, they turn abruptly. Roads pass the Huacas de los Cañafistoles and de los Mayorgas parallel to the main orientation of their constructions. The roads are between 2 and 3 m wide, flat, and not convex. Such roads are said to have reached almost to the Pacific coast. They are particularly numerous in the vicinity of Las Huacas, which seems to have been the center of the ancient Nicoya population. This assumption appears confirmed by the presence of a huge cemetery that has furnished an extraordinarily rich archaeological yield for a number of years and will continue to do so for many more.

Father Velasco, the priest of Santa Cruz on the Nicoya peninsula, made an agreement with Antonio Carrillo whereby he acquired the right to excavate at this place until 1902. Velasco has procured a rich and very valuable collection from here, and he continues to increase it with renewed excavations. According to Carrillo, this large cemetery of Las Huacas had neither walls nor other constructions of any kind. It was a plain piece of ground, differentiated from the surrounding area solely by sherds and broken metates. One day the

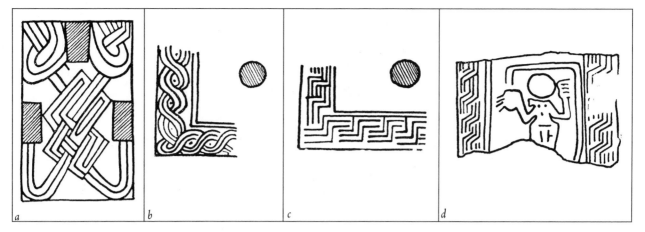

Figure 8.2
Sketches of
decoration on the
undersides of
metates, Las
Huacas

metate of Carrillo broke and he got the idea to dig at that spot in hopes of finding an unbroken one. This indeed happened; in fact, he found not only one but a number of metates with which he began a lively trade, a business that has now passed into the hands of Velasco. Before that, metates were imported from Nicaragua. Now the importation from Nicaragua is limited to manos because they are only infrequently found in the Las Huacas cemetery.

The buried human remains are found at about 80 cm below ground level at the large cemetery of Las Huacas; they extend down to a depth of 1 to 2 m. The bones of the dead have generally completely disappeared; usually only the teeth remain, although occasionally one can find a cranium or a few bones in fair condition. It is impossible to define the particular orientation in which the people were buried or the order of deposition where several were interred together. Most burials appear to have been of three or four individuals, one on top of the other. Next to the head one usually finds small jadeite figurines in the shape of small, knife-like, elongated lithic objects upon which a figure is usually indicated by straight incised lines. Often instead of jadeite they used other silicates of lighter color, at times with micaceous matter. Furthermore, one finds great masses of small ceramic jars, as well as small ceramic urns (tinajas) covered with stone axes.

Occasionally, large, very beautiful ceramic vessels have turned up, each with three specially decorated feet; in northern Middle America vessels often have three feet. The technical level of these Costa Rican vessels is inferior to that of the Aztecs or the Maya but is nevertheless remarkably high. Decoration on these ceramics consists of special human and animal figures, frequently with geometric elements, among which meandering lines are particularly popular. At times mineral coloring materials (red and brown) have been found in the form of little balls; these were presumably the same materials with which the ancient Indians painted their bodies, just as the Costa Rican Indians still do at the present time.

Stone axes of all sizes are common, most of them beautifully smoothed. Many polished quartz pieces were also found, and these may have been used to smooth the ceramic vessels. Beads of jadeite, quartz, or clay silicates show up occasionally. Portraits of their gods in copper are rather rare; even rarer are objects of gold. Since these are only found in the upper layers, the presumption is justified that the art of gold working took hold in Nicoya only at a late date, unless all gold objects were imported. Some of the gold objects found in Nicoya are in the National Museum of Costa Rica and should soon be reported in detail. They are mostly representations of animals (deer, alligators, most frequently eagles) or humans; often one also finds simple little pieces of gold leaf. Some time ago the skeleton of a female was unearthed whose cranium was totally covered with thin gold leaf. Some art objects are made of worked solid gold, others of gold wire. The present floor of the cemetery of Las Huacas is not level, but often shows low spots, places where the most beautiful jadeite objects have been found.

The vast majority of the objects found at this cemetery are metates of the three-footed type used

Figure 8.3
Antiquities from
the Bay of Fonseca

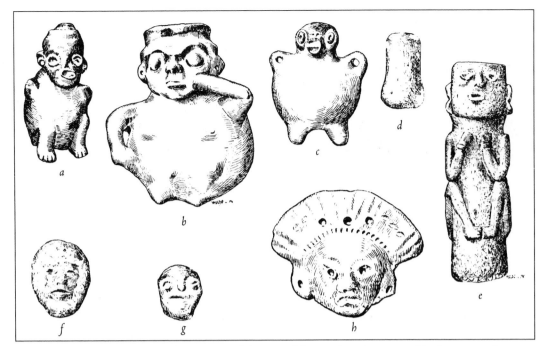

in northern Middle America. The metates of the highlands of Costa Rica and of the province of Chiriquí stand on four feet. The Las Huacas metates are different from those of northern Middle America, however, because here the two side feet are located almost in the middle of the metate, not at its corners (figure 8.2a). Also, the feet of the Las Huacas examples are different, usually taller with a round cross section; furthermore, they are curved and still thinner than in the north. The manos are round (in cross section), often worked down on one side, and longer than the width of the metate.

Decoration on these metates is normally limited to the outer margins of the underside; only occasionally is it extended to the rim of the upper side. Meandering lines or schematized animals are the most common decorations; quite often, one can find the intertwined band motif (figure 8.2a, b). Unfortunately, the local foreman of Father Velasco was so particular in guarding his employer's property rights that he would not even allow me to make sketches of some of these decorations. For this reason I could sketch only a few broken pieces (figure 8.2a–d).

Besides the large cemetery of Las Huacas, Carrillo believes that he has found another one, which, however, has not yet been investigated. He led me to the spot that is the same as the location of the two large limestone blocks previously mentioned. Other than a large amount of sherds, nothing else is remarkable about this place, and so I cannot be sure that it actually was another cemetery.

The original inhabitants of the Nicoya peninsula were the Chorotegas, who belong to the Mangue family. The Nicoya Chorotegas are close relatives of the Mangues or Dirians, who lived in the Sierra de Managua and Masaya in Nicaragua and only recently died out. The Nicoya Chorotegas are also related to the Chorotegas or Cholutecas, who lived near the Bay of Fonseca but died out a long time ago, and to the Chiapanecos, whose few survivors are still living in the few villages in the state of Chiapas. It would be of great interest to compare the culture of the Chorotegas of Nicoya with that of their relatives. To the best of my knowledge, however, archaeological investigations of those areas of Chiapas, Honduras, and Nicaragua are still very much neglected; thus, a far-reaching comparison is impossible. Even so, a few remarks may be in order.

As regards the old inhabitants of Chiapas (Chiapanecos), I cannot recall any characteristic particulars of their archaeological remains that are duplicated or similar to those of the Chorotegas of Nicoya. I can, however, say with certainty that the Chiapas inhabitants were completely distinct from their southern relatives in the art of building or architecture, because they had advanced to the construction of larger cities and of individual impressive structures with step construction (as I learned from *Publications of the Royal Museum of Ethnology in Berlin*, volume IV, book 1).[2]

I have already discussed this in detail elsewhere. The style of architecture used by the Chiapanecos differs considerably from that of the majority of the tribes of northern Middle America. The Chiapaneco style is characterized by a perpendicular step construction, that of the other groups by an obliquely rising step construction with a narrow upper landing. Unquestionably, the Chiapanecos who had emigrated from Nicaragua to Chiapas had been led quickly to a higher level of architectural development by following the example of their more advanced new neighbors.

During my trips in the area of the Bay of Fonseca, I have seen neither archaeological finds nor remains of ancient villages or buildings of the Cholutecas. The only antiquities I have seen that are said to come from the neighborhood of the Bay of Fonseca are owned by Messrs. J. Rössner & Co in Amapala (figure 8.3a–h). Their rough execution and their motifs do not remind me in the slightest of the antiquities of Nicoya. They might originate with the Lenca people since they are reminiscent of clay figurines from eastern El Salvador, as well as from the Department of Sensuntepeque (Cabañas) in the collection of Justo Armas in San Salvador.

I have seen relatively few antiquities of the Dirian and Mangues of Nicaragua. I reproduce some decorations on a flat, open ceramic vessel with three feet that was found in the vicinity of Masaya (figure 8.4). The designs are rather peculiar and may be ascribed to the Mangues; the roughly indicated motif of intertwined ribbons (figure 8.4b, c) reminds me somewhat of the style of the Chorotegas. The majority of the antiquities one can see in Nicaragua come from the Nahua settlements at Lake Nicaragua and from the neighboring Pacific coast. The single larger Indian settlement that I have seen near Masaya on the western side of the beautiful Lake Apoyo must also be of Nahua provenience. It consists of a number of terraces climbing up a hill with poorly preserved mounds in a north-south row; these are only clearly visible when the area has recently been cleaned or burned. The area is remarkable due to the numerous sculptured, but mostly fragmentary, monuments of human figures with rounded, smooth lower ends, which appear to have been sunk into the ground. The best preserved rather large figure is a human, on whose back sits a large four-legged monster with a huge mouth full of

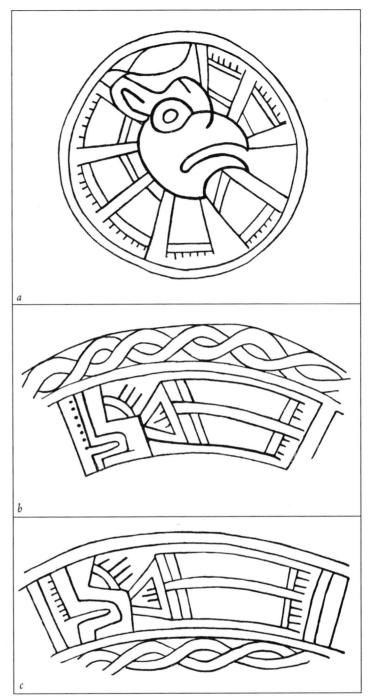

Figure 8.4
Designs on a
vessel from
Masaya:
a, interior base;
b, interior wall;
c, exterior wall.

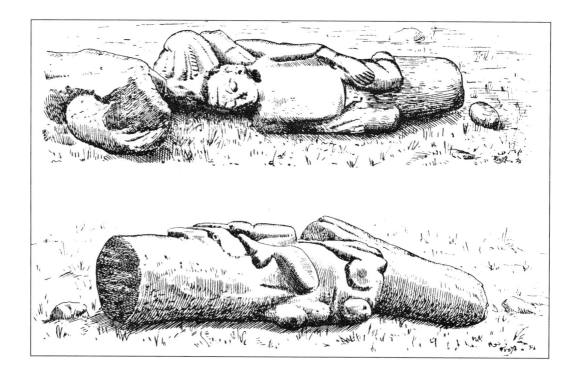

Figure 8.5 Stone figures from ruins on the western shore of Lake Apoyo

Figure 8.6 Petroglyph from Santa Clara, Nicaragua. Scale 1:12

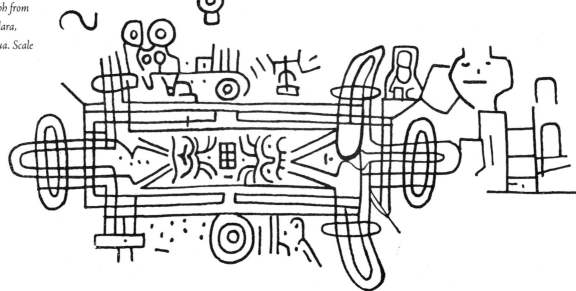

Figure 8.7 Petroglyph from Santa Clara, Nicaragua. Scale 1:12

sharp teeth (figure 8.5).

On a trip to the southern slope of the Sierra Managua I never saw a single old Indian settlement, but I did see some very interesting petroglyphs, which are located near San Rafael del Sur on steep rock walls of volcanic tuff alongside the brook of Santa Clara (figures 8.6, 8.7). Because of the dark color of the background the incisions are not always clearly visible and my sketches are therefore not very precise. Many years ago Dr. Flint made an exact copy of this rock art, but since I did not know whether this had been published, I felt that I should do some freehand sketches in order to document the petroglyphs. On one of them, the frequently used Nicoya motif of intertwined ribbons is clearly shown. I am told that similar petroglyphs can be found in the Piedra Pintada cave of San Andres near Masachapa; there are larger remains of Indian settlements in the Potrero La Cañada (pasture; cattle ranch) near Masachapa and stone sculptures at Citalapa. The rock art of the Matagalpa area of northern Nicaragua is quite different from the foregoing: for instance, that of the Letrero at Datauli in the Department of Jinotega (figure 8.8).

The Chorotegas of Nicoya had settled the largest part of the province of Guanacaste; a different tribe must have lived in the southeast of that province since a different type of building is found there. I could see this at a huaca at the Río Higuerón near the Cerro Pelado in the Las Cañas district (figure 8.9). Here a small round building is remarkable, adjoining a fairly large area that is covered with field stones, although not clearly delineated. At some distance from it are two parallel walls, also built up from uncut field stones; somewhat farther northwest was a small stone pavement on a low mound.

Even the most cursory view clearly shows the great difference between these simple constructions and those of the huacas of Nicoya. For one thing the walls do not enclose a courtyard. Here we find a circular construction that is reminiscent of the round huts of the Indians of Talamanca and of the numerous circular outlines of ancient Indian architectural remains at Buenos Aires in southern Costa Rica, which Pittier had found in his numerous expeditions.

Figure 8.8 Pictograph at Letrero near Datauli, Nicaragua. From a sketch by Max Schrecker. Scale 1:1

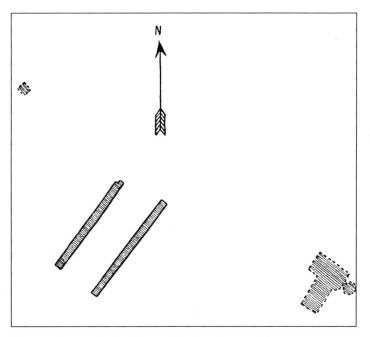

Figure 8.9 Huaca at the Río Higuerón, Las Cañas district. Scale 1:1050

NOTES

1. Sapper used the spelling "Carillo" but the family name and the ceramic type name derived from it are spelled Carrillo.
2. The specific reference has not been determined.

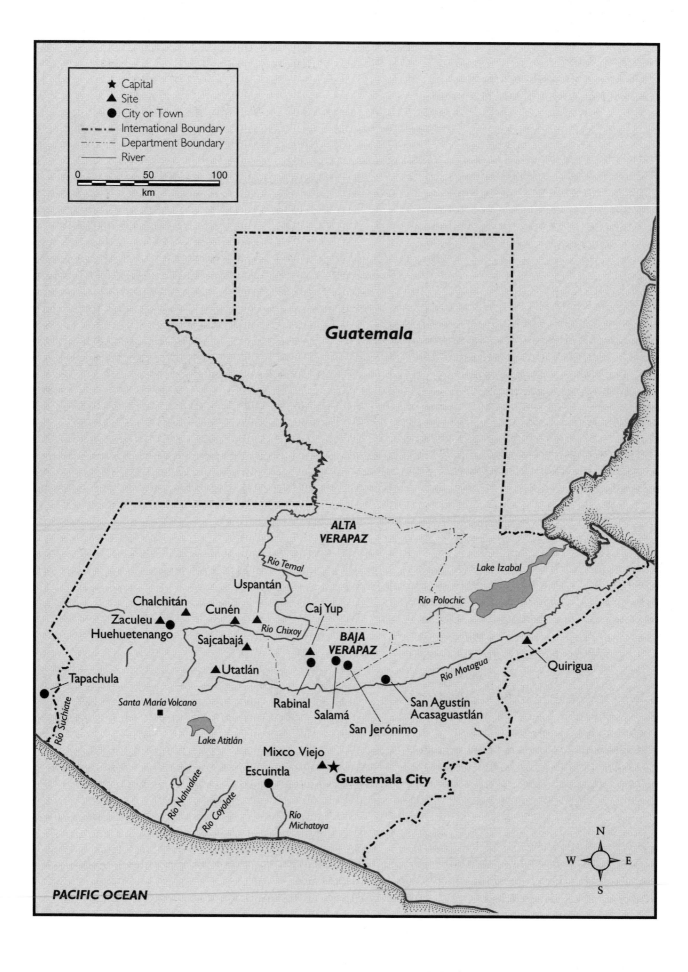

Capital
Site
City or Town
International Boundary
Department Boundary
River

0   50   100
km

Guatemala

**ALTA
VERAPAZ**

Río Temal

Lake Izabal

Uspantán

Río Polochic

Chalchitán

Cunén   Caj Yup

Zaculeu

Huehuetenango   *Río Chixoy*   **BAJA
VERAPAZ**

Sajcabajá

Quirigua

▲Utatlán

Río Motagua

Tapachula

Rabinal   San Agustín
Acasaguastlán

Salamá

Santa María Volcano   San Jerónimo

Río Suchiate

Lake Atitlán

Mixco Viejo

Escuintla   **Guatemala City**

Río Nahualate

Río Coyolate

Río Michatoya

N
W   E
S

PACIFIC OCEAN

CHAPTER 9

Importance of Pipils
in the Cultural Formation of Guatemala

Franz Termer

Originally published as
"Die Bedeutung der Pipiles für die Kulturgestaltung in Guatemala"
Baessler-Archiv 19(1936):108–113
Berlin: Verlag von Dietrich Reimer

COMMENTARY

I first studied this essay by Franz Termer about twenty years ago when I began my research on the Pipils of Central America. It speaks for its time, considering that very little was known archaeologically about the Pipils, and most of the information on which scholars had to rely came from the historical sources. Although the paper bears many errors of fact and interpretation, it is important because Termer emphasized that the Pipils played an important role in the culture history of Central America. Because the paper is based on a series of unfounded speculations and because it arrives at many mistaken conclusions, it must, however, be handled with care.

I will summarize some of the problems in Termer's interpretations, not to criticize him or his approach, which was based on the Kulturkreis school with its emphasis on the study of cultural distributions in relation to natural areas, but to show how much progress has been made in the study of the preconquest Pipils. We know now, for example, that "Achi" really does refer to the highland Maya dialects of Kaqchikel, K'iche', and Tz'utujil, and the term is not to be equated with "Pipil." When Father Ponce stated that some of the Achi of San Salvador spoke Pipil, what he meant was that they were bilingual.

Termer's reconstruction of the distribution of the Pipils in preconquest Guatemala has many errors.

Pipils were resettled in Salamá by Licenciado Cerrato after they were freed from slavery in 1548. The Acasaguastlan Pipils probably also settled there after the conquest. A more serious problem is Termer's totally unfounded argument that the Pipils were the source of the Mexican cultural elements among the highland Maya groups.

Nevertheless, some of the ideas in this essay still merit careful consideration. Termer perpetuated Lehmann's argument that the Pipil migrations occurred in several stages. We have now shown that was indeed what happened in El Salvador. Termer's emphasis on the importance of kin groups in maintaining social unity among the migrating Pipil groups foreshadows my own argument that the migrations were organized and led by Pipil noble houses similar to the noble lineages (*tecpan* or *tecalli*) of highland Mexico.

A central point that Termer makes several times—and one that is still true—concerns the need for more archaeological research on the Pipils to achieve a better understanding of their migrations and culture. This call was heeded by Termer's student Wolfgang Haberland and, more recently, by myself and others. It is my hope, or at least my fancy, that if Termer could somehow assess the state of Pipil archaeology today, he would be mightily impressed with the progress we have made.

—*William R. Fowler*

Importance of Pipils in the Cultural Formation of Guatemala

The interior highland regions of northern Central America have been widely assumed to be the home of the Maya people in terms of population affiliation and cultural conditions. They were called highland Maya to distinguish them from the culturally superior Maya who inhabited the Atlantic lowlands. Recent travel books that report on these regions don't reveal any detailed knowledge of the population and its culture and speak only of the Maya Indians of Guatemala. These books don't even mention the inhabitants of El Salvador, probably because, except for those few who live in out-of-the-way places, they had lost their racial and ethnic identity .

The scientific literature, as well as the chroniclers of the sixteenth century, recognized that besides the inhabitants belonging to the Maya family, other people lived in Guatemala and El Salvador, a people who were especially differentiated from the Maya by their languages. At least in the older reports, the linguistic differences were pointed out as significant because of the disappearance of these non-Maya tribes and because such linguistic differences were their only well-established characteristics. Modern research regarding former ethnographic conditions in northern Central America has therefore been heavily concerned with linguistic studies. One has only to remember the works of H. Berendt, Otto Stoll, and W. Lehmann, along with the important and masterful linguistic research of the K'iche' and Pipils of El Salvador by Schultze Jena.

The documentary sources of Spanish colonial times regarding the non-Maya elements are almost exclusively concerned with the Pipils. These are mostly reports dealing with the Mexican culture, and only a few are exclusively concerned with Guatemala and its adjacent areas. In contrast, the small number of contributions by indigenous writers of the time of the conquest are that much more important as they preserve old pre-Hispanic folk traditions, most of them written in Maya languages. As usual myth, legend, and historic truth are all mixed together. Getting to the historical truth for Guatemala is particularly difficult but not hopeless if one is willing to undertake a detailed investigation of the respective territory along with the study of sources.

Brasseur de Bourbourg was the first who worked along these lines, but his research does not form a reliable base in the light of modern exacting scholarship, and his reports need to be checked out at each locality. It is, however, not necessary to review the literature regarding the Pipils, since Lehmann (1920, 2:1059 ff.) has done so exhaustively.

This article will attempt to assess the significance of the Pipils vis-à-vis their neighbors in Guatemala along with considerations that occurred to me during my trip there. I am not concerned with

Pipil Glossary

Word	Spelling in original	English
achi	achi	Man, human being, master, noble
mumus	mumuz	Altar (mumus thought to be derived from Nahuatl *momoztli*)

Nahuatl Glossary

Word	Spelling in original	English
pipil, pipiltin	pipil, pipiltin	Prince or noble; boy
tecpan, tecalli		Noble lineages

linguistic research already accomplished by the aforementioned scholars whose objectives are to determine the ethnic relationship of the Pipils. Rather, my task here will be to establish the position of the Pipils within the cultural pattern of Guatemala with emphasis on archaeological, historical, and geographic concerns.

The following are securely established facts about the Pipils in terms of their areas of settlement, provenience, language, and culture.

THEIR SETTLEMENT AREAS IN NORTHERN CENTRAL AMERICA

At the time of conquest they lived in enclosed enclaves in the Pacific coastal lowlands of Guatemala, between the Río Coyolate and Río Michatoya (Squier 1858:317),* and in the Pacific lands of El Salvador, as well as in the inland districts of the Motagua Valley and the Salamá Basin. These settlement areas are identified by linguistic reports from older sources and by linguistic remains preserved into the nineteenth and twentieth centuries. It is surprising that the missionaries who reported on the last two districts never mentioned the Pipils, although fairly important mission establishments were located at Salamá and at San Jerónimo, as well as at San Agustín Acasaguastlán.

---

*   Squier places their western border at Río Nahualate, very probably for archaeological reasons. The differing reports by Ximénez (1721-22:69) and Alonso Ponce (1872, T. 57:326) do not correspond to the facts.

THEIR PROVENIENCE

All of the early authors uniformly call the Pipils immigrants from Mexican regions. Modern researchers, especially Lehmann and Schultze Jena, see them as descended from the older Nahua people of the highlands of Mexico, who were the bearers of the high pre-Aztec culture and who spoke an older Nahuatl dialect than did the Aztecs. Accordingly, the Pipils are but immigrant Toltecs, an opinion that agrees with that of Mendieta (1870), Torquemada (1723), and other early authors (Lehmann 1920). Even though the probability of these connections is great, archaeological substantiation in Guatemala is needed for its secure acceptance. Furthermore, we do not know whether the name *Pipils* was that of a tribe or rather a collective denomination of several populations, all of which were immigrants from Mexico.

THEIR LANGUAGE

The language of the Pipils has become thoroughly known through earlier research but especially through the more recent work of Schultze Jena. Thus, on the basis of its structure and location, it can definitely be related to the Nahuatl dialects of Mexico. Some other authors have confused Pipil with Nahuatl, which first came into Guatemala as a vernacular with the conquistadores. When, for example, Fuentes y Guzmán (1882, 1:203) asserts that a chair in "Pipil" has been established at the University of Guatemala (San Carlos), he really means "Nahuatl."

THEIR CULTURE

The Pipil culture is indicated by the scant remarks of earlier authors and accordingly leans closely to the religious belief of Mexico. Hartman (1907) and Schultze Jena (1933) have been able to show themes reminiscent of Mexican tales and legends still existing among the Pipils of El Salvador. We are least informed about their material culture. Since the older authors give us little information, only modern archaeological research can help us there. Such research, however, is in its infancy in

Guatemala, as has been shown in another article (Termer 1935).

Our entire secure knowledge of the Pipils consists only of their provenience, their foreign character in northern Central America, and their relations to the Mexican Nahua people. We do not know their relations with their neighbors in Guatemala and El Salvador (that is, the highland Maya and other isolated tribes of those regions). The time of immigration of the Pipils into Central America is not known for sure nor are its routes. We also do not know about the relationships among the several geographically and temporally distinct Pipil enclaves. The following remarks are limited, because of space considerations, to the Pipils in the interior of highland Guatemala.

The reports of the sixteenth and seventeenth centuries regarding other than Maya inhabitants in northern Central America mention the Pipils only as a people of the Pacific lowlands. In comparison, the Achies are mentioned in the highlands. Las Casas was apparently the first to refer to "la gente que llamaban los Achies que por las sierras habitaban (the people called Achies that inhabited the sierras)."[1] They were referred to as cannibals, which is probably in connection with religious ceremonies following Aztec examples. Torquemada also speaks of Achies in Guatemala, who owned pictorial codices in which the biblical flood was shown, but which were destroyed by the missionaries (1723, Lib. XV Cap. 49; T. 3:134). The language of the Achies is said to be that of the people of Guatemala, and probably following las Casas, the Achies are claimed to be inhabitants of the highlands (Torquemada 1723, Lib. XX Cap. 70, T. 3:553; Lib. XIV Cap. 26: T. 2:584). Torquemada has taken this description verbatim from Mendieta (1870, Lib. IV Cap. 41:539).[2]

The word achi belongs to the Maya languages of the highlands where it means "man, human being, master, noble." The Nahuatl word pipil has a double meaning. It can mean "boy," but it can also mean "prince, noble." This double meaning can be perceived from the study of the early authors of Guatemala who use the word alternatively in one meaning or the other. Torquemada, for instance, speaks of the "Pipiltin" as "principales y nobles (princes and nobles)," Fuentes y Guzmán of the "Pipils" as "muchachos (boys)." While Torquemada is writing about the tribes resident in the highlands, Fuentes y Guzmán (1882) refers to the lowland Pipils near Escuintla. The *Isagoge Histórico Apologético* also applies the meaning of muchachos in reference to the lowland Pipils (1892:313). In both cases the group's original Mexican provenience is emphasized, meaning that both are Nahua people.

Considering the distribution of the highland tribes, we must not judge their earlier extension just from the scarce remains of their language, which has persisted until most recent times. It cannot be assumed that they were limited to the basin of Salamá and a few locations in the Motagua Valley. There were most likely areas to the west of Salamá where their language was no longer preserved in colonial times. In the high basin of Rabinal there is infallible proof that originally Mexican elements lived there at one time. In this area are large complexes of ruins that are identical in their architectural style to those that were known to pre-Aztec inhabitants of the highland valley of Mexico. Furthermore, the present inhabitants of Rabinal and its surroundings call themselves *achi* in the currently exclusively spoken K'iche' language and are called the same by their neighbors in the western K'iche' area.

In this context it must be noted that among the buildings of the ruins of Caj Yup is a round altar which to this day is called *mumus* by the Indians. Lehmann found the same word in the vocabulary of the Pipils of Acasaguastlán and supposed that it is a parallel to the Nahuatl *momoztli* (Lehmann 1920:1070, #22). Thus, I believe his conclusion is verified.

It follows that the Maya dialects of the highlands use the word *achi* in place of the Nahuatl word *pipil* in the sense of "master, noble, principal," and it is quite possible that this is a direct Maya translation of the Nahuatl word insofar as *achi* is used as the name of a tribe. In this way we must not be deceived by the sixteenth-century reports. Alonso Ponce, a reliable author who traveled widely in Middle America, considers *achi* as a collective term for the highland Maya of Central

Guatemala, namely the K'iche', Kaqchikel, and Tz'utujil. He also mentioned that some residents among the Pipil Indians, living in the city of San Salvador, were achies but spoke the Pipil language (Ponce 1872:383, 400, 426–427).[3]

From these sources two possibilities emerge: achies are the Maya tribes of the central highlands of Guatemala or they are the separate Pipil inhabitants of the highlands who must have entered into a special relationship with the Maya tribes there. Furthermore, the remarks are important in connection with the *Rabinal Achi* drama and the *Popol Vuh*. In the title of the former, the *achi* is used with the meaning of "prince" or "king." The person refers in his speeches repeatedly to his weapons that came from the Toltecs (Brasseur de Bourbourg 1862). In both texts the reigning royal families are called *yaqui*, a name for immigrants of the Nahua tribes from Mexico, as earlier authors, including Seler, have pointed out.

In our survey of the highlands of western Guatemala we could find among many ruins other traces of this people, such as in the region of the K'iche', the province of the Kaqchikel, in the Poqoman, as well as the eastern parts of the Mam area. Among the relatively better preserved ruins I will cite only those of Sajcabajá, Uspantán, Cunén, Huehuetenango, and Mixco Viejo.

Even Utatlán, despite its destruction, shows indications that the style of its buildings and many architectural peculiarities have commonality with the other places. Farther west, beyond the K'iche' drainages, only Zaculeu and Chalchitán show strong similarities with the other ruins. Otherwise, the western region of Guatemala has only simple earthworks and tumuli that are distributed throughout the Mam area but can also be found in other parts of Guatemala.

Accordingly, an area can be determined, defined in the west, north, and south by the architectural similarity showing Mexican influence. In the east I have not been able to define a boundary because my visits to those regions have been too rare to allow me to judge them. Unfortunately, we do not have sufficient archaeological reports about minor finds, because excavations have not been executed in a scientifically competent manner. Even

so, I have seen small items in private collections which, in their style, leaned heavily on models from the highlands of Mexico.

Along with the early authors, we are in the habit of considering the polities of the K'iche', Kaqchikel, and Tz'utujil as empires of the highland Maya. It is presumed that the founding and development of these powerful states can be credited to the indigenous Maya tribes. Since the Maya language was spoken there at the time of the conquest, this opinion was formed then. This assumption is not proven, however, because foreign conquerors and culture bearers have often taken on the language of the conquered populations, especially if they no longer had contact with their former home and became intermingled with their vassals. The ruling class may have preserved its language longer. We do not know anything about all of that from the Guatemalan highlands. The probability exists that the Nahua immigrants settled as masters among the Maya of the highlands, founded political states there, and incorporated the Maya into these polities.

Most likely the Maya population at that time was larger in the western K'iche' area than in present day Baja Verapaz. This may be the reason why the Pipil language persisted longer in Baja Verapaz than in the K'iche' region. Here living conditions were favorable in the *tierra fría* (highlands) as the sparse forests allowed good possibilities for settlement. At Rabinal and Salamá there were, however, dry interior basins with normally sparsely vegetated steppes that had to be irrigated for intensive agriculture.* These environmental conditions made the area less favorable for dense settlement. It is possible therefore that immigrants could be more sealed off than in the west and thus hold on to their language longer. The advance of the K'iche' language into the basin of Rabinal could have been caused by the wars of the K'iche' empire against that of Rabinal, although it may only have taken place during colonial times, when *reducciones* (centralized commu-

---

* I cannot tell whether the highland Maya were familiar with irrigation or received that knowledge only from the Mexican Nahua people.

nities) were quickly imposed in the Baja Verapaz (see chapter 2, this volume). As a result of these reducciones, Indians from more distant regions may at times also have been settled there. It is impossible for me to know whether the still preserved *Título Rabinal* contains information about historical events, since the village authorities refused to let me see it.

If we assume that the immigrants stopped using the Nahuatl language in favor of the local Guatemalan Maya dialects, we must also assume that the number of these new immigrants was not very large, but that they succeeded in making themselves the masters of the highland Maya on account of their cultural superiority. Without reinforcements from their original home, their ethnicity succumbed to the Maya inhabitants. The master caste in possession of the political and spiritual leadership preserved its old traditions such as their successors have later retained, even though they themselves were only able to communicate in K'iche' or Kaqchikel.

Thus, codices were made up of legends of descent and migrations along with religious content. And while not a single one of them has surfaced from the highlands of Guatemala, we do have an explanatory text in the *Título de los Señores de Totonicapán* translated into the Spanish language (Recinos 1950). Similarly, Lehmann has called the *Popol Vuh* "an interpretation of a pictorial codex within a framework of traditions" (1906b:224 ff.).

We must think of the immigration into highland Guatemala in terms of separate movements. The social structure of the Mexican people, with strong emphasis on family ties, made it probable that the tribes and clans would be united during their migrations and that they would move in small groups. The geographical features of the areas through which their migration led them were also unfavorable for a massive population movement, while the central basins and valleys of the highlands of Guatemala provided ideal conditions for settlement. These areas were also very similar geographically and physically to their homelands in the Mexican highlands, that is, with regard to altitude, climate, forestation, and water availability. Thus, their mode of living remained the same in their new surroundings as in their former home region.

It is not surprising that the Toltec migrants settled in the Guatemalan highlands and took roots with their culture, something that seems to indicate that the highland Maya culture was inferior to their own. When the ties to Mexico were broken, sometime after the demise of the Toltec empire, the transplanted culture remained as an offshoot that had fruitful effects upon the Maya population of the highlands but would not, over time, develop new impulses.

The traditions speak of an original consolidated empire of the Toltec immigrants into Guatemala. Shortly thereafter, it broke into partial dominions with different overlords, who started feuding with one another and weakened their aggressive political power. Thus, we must think of a number of small principalities in the highlands of Guatemala during the last century before the Spanish conquest, whose rulers were of Toltec origin, each with its own political and cultural center.

This picture has been developed by pursuing traditionally reported historical events from native sources and will remain valid as long as archaeological evidence can support it. Would it not be a logical explanation for the still enigmatic parallel appearance all over highland Guatemala of remains of high artistry with clearly Mexican influence along with the occurrence of a crude ceramic ware, poorly elaborated artistically (Lothrop 1933)? The few previously undertaken scientific excavations have shown this parallel repeatedly. This fact appears to speak emphatically against the concept of a *cultura arcaica* (archaic culture) in the area.

We do not have firm information about the path of Nahua migrations to and within Guatemala. The place-names in the indigenous sources do not give such indications; in part, they refer to the names of mythical localities; in part, to local areas of the K'iche' region, which can rarely be identified. The interpretations of Brasseur de Bourbourg are unreliable and need to be double-checked. Since the migrating routes have been treated elsewhere (Termer 1934), I refer the reader to that publication.

Our deductions have pointed up a number of problems that are of importance for the understanding of the cultural development of highland Guatemala and are intimately connected with the problem of the Pipils. We agree with other investigators that the lowland Pipils of the Pacific slope belong to an older branch of the Mexican Toltec population and must also be separated from the highland Pipils chronologically. The events of the conquest also show indications from the *Título de los Señores de Totonicapán* that the two were independent of each other, spatially and politically, and that the Pacific coastal Pipil empire was separated from the highland states. We cannot discuss this any further. In any event, more intensive archaeological research in Guatemala can give very important clues about the relation of the Pipils with the Maya within the development of the culture of northern Central America. Such research can perhaps put into a new light the "question of the Maya" in the highlands, while presently we can only theorize about it.

Notes

1. Termer gives his source for the las Casas quote as *Apológetica Historia*, Kap. 205 (Doc. inéd. T. 66 [1876] S. 511). Charles Gibson (1975:399) in his *Handbook of Middle American Indians* article, however, states that three complete editions of this work were published in 1909, 1958, and 1967. Gibson discussing various collections of Documentos Inéditos states "a large amount of las Casas material, including his *Historia de las Indias* (is) in volumes 62–66" (1973:14). Thus, the quotation cited may refer to a passage in either of the works by las Casas.

2. Termer includes in this citation "ed. Madrid 1870, S. 539)." However, Burrus (1973:146) says that the "*Historia* was unpublished until 1870, when it was first issued in Mexico City by Joaquín García Icazbalceta." Thus, "ed. Madrid" was probably an error in the original.

3. Termer describes Ponce as the author of *Relación breve*, but Warren (1973:60) says "the two friars who accompanied him successively as his secretaries noted down the incidents of his travels. . . . It is generally accepted that the two secretaries were Alonso de San Román and Antonio de Ciudad Real." Bibliographers variably cite the author of *Relación breve* as either Ponce or Ciudad Real.

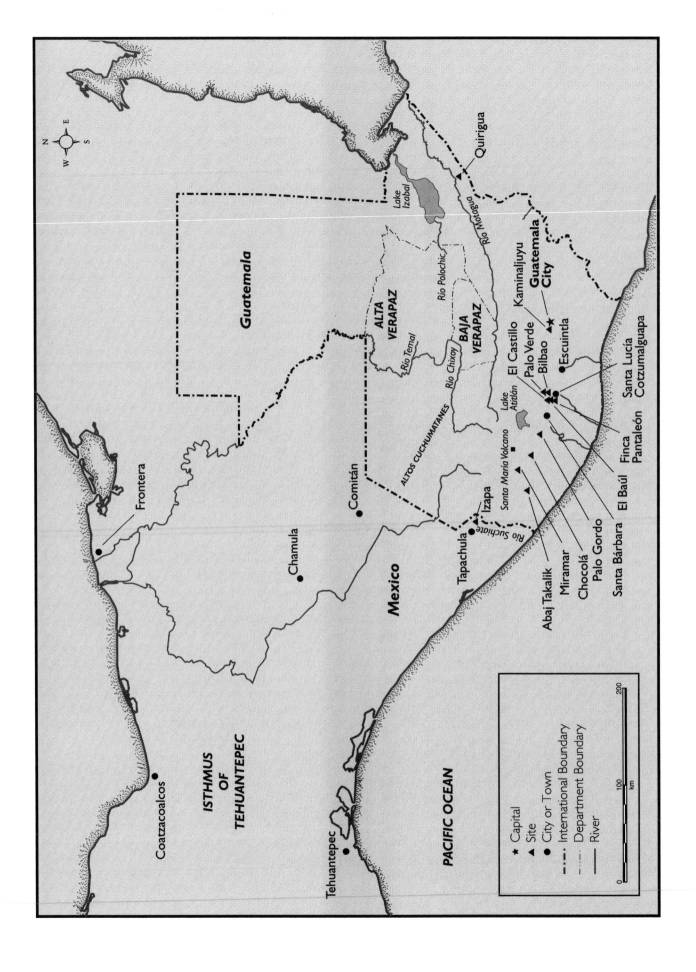

CHAPTER 10

Travel Letter from Puerto Mexico

Walter Lehmann

Originally published as
"Reisebrief vom 18. Januar aus Puerto Mexiko"
Zeitschrift für Ethnologie 58(1926):171–177
Berlin: Museum für Völkerkunde

Commentary

As one who has spent virtually his entire professional life engaged in archaeological research in Pacific coastal Guatemala, I have always had a keen interest in the early explorers. A good introduction to them is contained in Parsons' report on the 1962-63 Bilbao excavations (Parsons 1967). It provides a brief history of exploration and research in the Cotzumalguapa area of Escuintla, Guatemala, that mirrors to a large extent the history of exploration in all of Pacific coastal Guatemala. In spite of his important contributions to knowledge of the area, Lehmann is not even mentioned. In this commentary, therefore, I will concentrate principally on Lehmann's Pacific coastal Guatemala experience and the direct link between many of his keen and far-sighted observations in 1925 and recent archaeological investigations. Remarkably, he met and/or commented on many who were involved in the early explorations and later excavations.

At the time of his visit very little was known of the complex prehistory of this region now characterized as a cultural corridor or crossroads. Practically all the work on the basic chronological and cultural sequences still lay ahead. While there were tantalizing bits and pieces of the cultural richness that he comments on, even the antiquity of Mesoamerican civilization was a mystery. Hardly anything was known of the basic archaeological sequences, the development of early complex societies, the first pottery, ceramic chronology, settlement patterns, the problem of the pot belly–style sculpture, or the important role of Kaminaljuyu in the rise of Maya civilization. The great effort by the Carnegie Institution of Washington with Kidder and Shook at Kaminaljuyu still lay twenty years in the future. When I look back on this period, I find it remarkable that while there had been a steady stream of visitors to the coastal region from the mid to late 1800s, no scientific excavations took place until Thompson's work at El Baúl in 1941 (Thompson 1948).

The excavations that took place at Chocolá about the time of Lehmann's visit to the site were anything but scientific (Burkitt 1930). Henry Kummerfeldt, the manager of the Finca Chocolá, is mentioned in the letter and was a good friend of Robert Burkitt who directed excavations at the site. In 1922, Kummerfeldt apparently gave Burkitt the important but fragmented Monument 1 that had been found while plowing among mounds at the site some time before. Burkitt promptly boxed it up for shipment to the University Museum, University of Pennsylvania, with whom he had a long-term contract to obtain antiquities. The monument has been at the museum ever since (Jones 1986). Burkitt also probably took photographs of the monument. He or Kummerfeldt must have shown Lehmann a copy of these photographs since Lehmann mentions seeing a photograph of a Maya relief fragment during his Chocolá visit and notes its similarity to a sculpture fragment from Miraflores near Guatemala City. Lehmann is undoubtedly referring to sculptures reported from the Finca Miraflores that comprised part of the Kaminaljuyu site. Lehmann's great powers of observation, background, and interest in Maya art are quite apparent in this instance since the Chocolá sculpture is in the Miraflores style and bears a great similarity to Stela 10 from Kaminaljuyu excavated thirty years later by Espinosa.

On entering Guatemala, Lehmann met Franz Termer who was then engaged in research in the Cuchamatanes mountain range of western Guatemala. This is yet another link between an early explorer and later research since Termer went on to excavate Palo Gordo, a large site in the piedmont zone of Suchitepequez with Cotzumalguapa-style sculpture. Unfortunately, Termer died before he could complete the excavation report. In 1995 Chinchilla, during his dissertation research in Germany, encountered the original Palo Gordo site plan in the Hamburg Ethnographic Museum. That plan revealed important details of Termer's excavations, including the original location of various monuments (Chinchilla 1996a).

While in Guatemala City, Lehmann observed various private collections and with wonderful foresight commented on the important Mexican influence on what is now known as Kaminaljuyu. These observations are based on only a single figurine head similar to those from Teotihuacán and on a probable Tohil Plumbate vessel with Mexican style elements. These observations predate the discovery of the Teotihuacán *talud-tablero*–style structures later uncovered at Kaminaljuyu.[1]

Lehmann briefly mentions Mr. Dieseldorff, thanking him for the opportunity to prepare sketches of several antiquities in his private collection. Erwin P. Dieseldorff was a member of a distinguished coffee-growing family of German immigrants with successful farms in the Alta Verapaz area of Guatemala. He was also an avid aficionado of archaeology and ethnography with various publications to his credit, as well as a major collector of antiquities. One of the most useful collections of whole vessels that I ever observed while working in the storeroom of the Guatemala National Museum was the superb Dieseldorff collection. Most of these pieces are from the northern highlands around Alta Verapaz. They are most valuable to the scholar and deserve to be published in their own right since they remain largely ignored and unknown. To Dieseldorff's credit, they were presented to the museum instead of languishing in a private collection.

There are several references to the Pipil style of the Cotzumalguapa region. The first is Lehmann's discussion of three stone reliefs located in the Astronomical Observatory in Guatemala City. He probably did not realize it, but the three monuments are Monuments 1 to 3 from the site of Palo Verde located north of the Cotzumalguapa capital zone of Bilbao-El Baúl on the Escuintla piedmont. They were transported to the city shortly after Seler's visit to the Palo Verde site in 1900 and were moved to various locations, including the Observatory, before finally being placed after 1948 in the National Museum. These are ballplayer stelae similar to, though not as finely carved as, the better known ballplayer monuments from Bilbao now at the Berlin Ethnographic Museum.

During Lehmann's era and later, there was a commonly held belief that the Pipil were migratory Nahuatl speakers from central Mexico—both originators of the Cotzumalguapa art style and responsible for the Cotzumalguapa archaeological culture. To some extent, Thompson's excavations at El Baúl in 1941 were directed toward linking possible earlier Pipil migrations into Guatemala with development of the Cotzumalguapa culture. It took Parsons' research at Bilbao in the 1960s to put the Pipil phenomenon to rest even though his work was flawed by attempts to link directly the development of the Cotzumalguapa archaeological culture to Teotihuacán and its assumed Middle Classic expansion onto the south coast of Guatemala.

On subsequent visits to the Cotzumalguapa area, Lehmann reports Stela 1 from El Castillo as well as other monuments then located in a courtyard of the Finca Pantaleón, now the Ingenio Pantaleón. This imposing monument carved on both sides, along with many other sculptures, is now located at the principal offices of Pantaleón, S.A., in Guatemala City. None of these has been recorded by the Instituto de Antropología e Historia de Guatemala, the governing body for cultural remains, but an excellent article including photographs was published recently discussing provenience and other details (Chinchilla 1996b).

Apparently during these same visits, Lehmann described the Piedra Herrera now commonly known as Stela 1 at El Baúl, first reported in 1923. The temporal placement of the sculpture with its hieroglyphic inscription is perhaps Lehmann's most important contribution in this report. He was the first to correctly read and interpret the inscription as an Initial Series date in the Maya calendar. The date of 7.19.7.8.12 12 Eb (AD 29 in the GMT correlation) was met with skepticism by Morley and Thompson since it fell much earlier than known lowland Maya monuments. Although the date has since been modified to 7.19.15.7.12 12 Eb 0 Ceh? (AD 37), it remains one of the few cycle 7 monuments known. Thompson denied its antiquity, stating that the monument probably dated to around AD 1100 to 1450 based on style. In part, this led to the 1941 excavations at El Baúl to obtain evidence of dating.

Stela 1 is located with the sculpture display at the Finca El Baúl. These sculptures are primarily from the El Baúl site and immediate surroundings but unfortunately many lack precise proveniences, having been discovered during agricultural activities. In the past several years the development of a new urban area, the Colonia Maya, has destroyed a significant portion of the newly discovered southern groups. In the process new sculptures have been discovered and, with several exceptions, are also in the Baúl sculpture display. A salvage archaeological operation was conducted in 1996 and 1997 within part of the area most disturbed by the housing development.

There have been many visitors to the Cotzumalguapa region since the mid-1800s but until very recently the visitor had a difficult time gaining access to the various sites and farms where the sculptures were located. Happily, the owner of the Bilbao site, Ricardo Muñoz, built a private museum in 1997 at the entrance to the Finca Las Ilusiones on the outskirts of Santa Lucía Cotzumalguapa and moved the bulk of the collection from the finca patio. He also transported several other sculptures that were unguarded at the Bilbao site and made fiberglass copies of those too large to move. These are all attractively displayed in the museum, which is open to the public. So, between the outdoor sculpture display at El Baúl and the Las Ilusiones museum it is now possible to gain a fair understanding of this enigmatic art style.

Lehmann comments further on the early stela found in the Finca Santa Margarita west of Chocolá and 18 km northwest of modern Retalhuleu in the upper piedmont region. The site complex is now known as Abaj Takalik. He described the Piedra Schlubach monument, now identified as Stela 2, as having an inscription belonging to cycle 7 or 8 and infers indirectly that it is similar to the early dated monument at El Baúl. Stela 2 clearly appears to be cycle 7, although erosion has removed any possibility of determining the exact date. The most likely dating is between 38 and 18 BC, based on its stylistic resemblance to Stela 1 at El Baúl. The date is supported by a corrected radiocarbon date of 102 BC±176 from carbon deposited below the monument. Another early monument, Stela 5 at Abaj Takalik, was recently discovered and has a cycle 8 date ranging from AD 83 to 126.

Lehmann noted the other cruder stone monuments found in the area of the Finca Isidro Piedra Parada (Abaj Takalik) that were probably pot belly sculptures. These are found widely distributed on the Pacific coast of Guatemala and adjacent highlands, principally at Kaminaljuyu, as well as in coastal El Salvador and at Izapa in Chiapas. They are the subject of much speculation as to their chronological placement and significance, although a recent thesis by Rodas (1993) and subsequent research by Chinchilla (1997) places them firmly in the Late Formative period.

Lehmann had a great interest in linguistics, and his letter is filled with comments about recording word lists in the various languages. One is Tánitóc, which he recorded in the vicinity of Tapachula, Chiapas, Mexico, commenting on its relation with Mixe-Zoque. We now know that Mixe-Zoque has great antiquity, with many loan words appearing in the Maya language family. Another hypothesis, although far from being universally accepted, is the relation of Mixe-Zoque with the Olmec archaeological culture. Some have even proposed a link between Mixe-Zoque speakers and the spread of the early Barra and Locona-Ocós pottery that some believe linked the Gulf coast with the Pacific coast of Chiapas and Guatemala. This comment indicates how remarkably prescient Lehmann turned out to be in so many areas.

In the more than seventy years since Lehmann's trip, the Pacific coast has seen many changes, some drastic. There have been urban developments, deforestation, agricultural intensification, agrarian reform, and attendant widespread destruction and massive looting of archaeological sites. There are, however, still large sites to discover, new sculptures to be uncovered, and new interpretations to be made of this dynamic region of ancient Middle America.

–Frederick J. Bove

Acknowledgment. I thank Dr. Elin Danien of the University Museum, University of Pennsylvania, and Dr. Oswaldo Chinchilla, Popol Vuh Museum, Guatemala, for help in the preparation of this commentary.

Travel Letter from Puerto Mexico

I am writing to inform you briefly of my present trip, while I await the steamer to take me from here[2] to Frontera in order to visit Palenque and continue the trip further on to Yucatán, where I will meet Dr. Morley at Chichén Itzá.

The trip via Havana to Veracruz was agreeable, although the last part was very hot. In Veracruz I saw a number of Huastec and Totonac stone antiquities, as well as a large, little-known *lienzo* (pictorial manuscript on cloth) from the early days of the conquest. It is covered with painted pictures that are explained by several glosses.

In Mexico City I found a number of new archaeological items. The remains of a temple in the neighborhood of the Cathedral are interesting because besides the buildings, which are apparently from several periods, important stone reliefs of figures partially painted in various colors belong to them. One can see on one of the preserved walls a relief of the head of a snake. Even if it is much smaller and cruder than the huge sculpted heads of the Quetzalcoatl temple at Teotihuacán, it is nevertheless undoubtedly stylistically related to them. That is one of the reasons why I believe this building of the Ciudadela is more recent than the smaller step-pyramid that stands in front of it with no relief decoration.

I hope to be able to investigate this important question at the site of Teotihuacán, since the director of the Anthropological Department of Mexico has kindly invited me to visit the site of Teotihuacán and specifically the Ciudadela with him. The local investigation in Teotihuacán resulted in a discovery of important circumstances of which I was up to then ignorant. Since the smaller stucco pyramid of the Ciudadela forms at one point a continuation of the other larger pyramid that is decorated with ornaments in the round, the larger pyramid has to be older than the smaller one. To judge by the broad Tláloc faces of the rough frescos that I saw for the first time in April of 1926, the smaller stucco pyramid of the Ciudadela has to be from a very late date.

I therefore do not need to change the date of the larger pyramid. I was able to study the rich collections in the *Museo Nacional* after having obtained special government permission to photograph them. I also obtained a photocopy of the *Historia de los Reinos de Colhuacán y de México*, which I had already encountered in 1909. This is written in the Nahuatl language and is an historically, as well as mythologically, interesting manuscript from the old Boturini collection (Lehmann 1906a).

The head of the Anthropological Department also invited me on an archaeological excursion to Iguala in the State of Guerrero. I was able to record a Nahuatl dialect there (at Chilapa), which differs in some respect from the Nahuatl of the Valley of Mexico.

My linguistic work was at first concerned with the question of the presence of tone-steps. I could already discern those in the Mixtec language, of which I started to compile a small vocabulary in Veracruz. In Mexico City I first investigated Otomí. This language has many tone-steps that give it its phonetic peculiarity, along with an unusual voiceless, nasal, breathy sound, which in German is called *Hauchlauten*.

I investigated several places in the Pedregal where geological as well as archaeological questions arose. Here Mr. Wörn was of great help. He owns a peculiar, round step-pyramid in the vicinity of Peña Pobre, whose lowest level is surrounded by a thick layer of lava. To get a clear picture of the geological conditions of that region, I collected samples of the various layers in the quarries of the Pedregal (not far from San Angel), for whose definite determination I will ask a professional geologist.

In these quarries one can observe in some places two heavy layers of lava, one above the other, but separated by other layers. In San Angel itself, specifically in Cupilco, one sees only one layer of lava, the lower one of the quarries. Under this at Cupilco was a special layer with ceramic sherds and human skeletons whose bones showed no trace of carbon; thus they were probably interred deliberately in this layer before the great influx of lava that covered it. Geologically these lava flows are recent, as they came from the neighboring Xictle (Xitle) volcano,[3] even though presently it is not possible to determine their definite age. Something geologically recent could, however, be archaeologically old. What I have seen so far of the Cupilco finds appear to belong to a rather primitive culture. I want to examine all of them once more in Mexico City, since I have seen only part of them.

I also studied a number of private collections in Mexico City. That of Mr. Genin appears to be the most important. I saw there a new type of clay tablet with grotesque, long-legged figures in the style of the Maya that comes from Palenque. I also saw a fine three-legged clay vessel covered on its outer side with stucco and the remains of colored painting, especially in turquoise-green color. It was also supposedly found in Palenque and is reminiscent of my finds at Teotihuacán. Since Seler had discovered Toltec paintings underneath fres-

cos of Maya hieroglyphs in Palenque, it is unavoidable to also judge this Palenque vessel in the Genin Collection as Toltec. This demonstrates that the related ceramics of Teotihuacán are also Toltec. Unfortunately, the origin of this vessel is no more archaeologically secure than the clay tablet decorated with the relief of a bird's head in the same collection; the latter is supposed to come from Chichén Itzá but looks as if it came from Teotihuacán.

I was able to procure for the Museum in Berlin two very peculiar stone sculptures of Totonac provenience. They are a type of which only very few pieces are known. I also visited the region of Azcapotzalco, an area rich in archaeological remains that are closely connected with Teotihuacán. Portrait incensarios from Azcapotzalco show a certain affinity with a group of Zapotec urns, as well as with large Aztec incensarios in the form of a figure, even though the latter are created in a less dynamic style. Coarser vessels of the so-called Zapotec funerary urn type can be found all the way to the Pacific slope of Guatemala.

At the beginning of November I traveled via Veracruz and Tapachula to Guatemala. Dr. Termer awaited me at the Río Suchiate, as Dr. Roderich Schlubach very kindly had arranged for us to meet there. Dr. Termer is presently visiting the far-flung Altos Cuchumatanes mountains.

Guatemala presented me with a rich menu of activities in linguistic as well as archaeological regards. Mr. Kummerfeldt, the manager of Chocolá, was most helpful; it is one of the properties of the house Schlubach-Sapper. I could acquire various dialects of the Maya language family that so far have been poorly investigated, as for instance the languages of Soloma, Aguacatán, Santa Bárbara, and so on. Tone-steps play an important role in Maya dialects; however, they do not dominate the language as much as in Otomí or Zapotec. The most noticeable characteristics of Maya languages are the so-called *letras heridas*,[4] which have evolved tone-historically.

So far as I can presently judge, these letras heridas appear to be ancient sounds, which have changed in part through the relaxation into their respective simple consonants, in part through palatalization into the respective affricates. It can be shown that the Huastec language has remained on the step of a certain tone modification, which connects it with only a part of the dialects of the Maya group. In this respect Huastec cannot be considered as one of the oldest Maya languages.

In the vicinity of Chocolá I saw a number of antiquities, among them stone yokes and the photograph of a fragment of a Maya relief figure, which is similar to a fragment from Miraflores near Guatemala City.

In the capital city of Guatemala I saw various private collections. A ceramic head of most delicate facial features comes from Miraflores. It is incredibly beautiful, a real work of art, but not of the Maya type, rather Mexican and reminiscent of certain little clay heads from Teotihuacán. A clay mug comes from there also; it has dark brown glaze and the relief figure of a warrior, similar to the vessels that Seler has described. Both pieces indicate an archaeologically important Mexican influence in the area of Guatemala's capital.

Mr. Dieseldorff deserves my thanks for giving me the opportunity to copy two outstanding antiquities, the sketches of which have been sent to Berlin. One of these is a clay vessel in the form of a bowl with twelve engraved figures along with hieroglyphs in the Maya style. The other is a stone bowl with the head of a buck and twelve engraved hieroglyphs, which are quite different from the Maya forms.

Three thick stone reliefs of the Pipil style of the Santa Lucía Cotzumalguapa region are located in the newly built Observatorio Astronómico of the capital. When they were lying in a cornfield near Guatemala City, I made rubbings of two of them for the Munich Museum in 1909. I have copied the third one now, thanks to the permission of the Minister of Agriculture, Sr. Salvador Herrera.

During an excursion to the famous ruins of Quiriguá, I saw on a hill the remains of a small stone construction along with two, unfortunately broken, stelae nearby. This was at a distance of a half-hour horseback ride and behind the hospital of the United Fruit Company. These stelae are made of weathered slate-type stone, smaller than the stelae at Quiriguá and covered with badly weathered hieroglyphic inscriptions. It shows that there are Maya ruins not only at the site of Quiriguá but also at some distance from it. These stelae are presumably older than those of Quiriguá. In Quiriguá I recorded the language of the Garifuna (black Caribs from St. Vincent) and was able to get two funerary songs.

Later on I was able to visit the antiquities of Pantaleón, El Castillo, and El Baúl, thanks to the kindness of Minister Sr. Salvador Herrera and Sr. Carlos Herrera. The stone monuments that are set up in the courtyard of Finca Pantaleón come from the region of the neighboring town of Santa Lucía Cotzumalguapa and are in the Pipil style. A pyramid is located near El Castillo, and at some distance from it is a huge stone block with a surface of 2.50 by 3.15 m and a thickness of 50 cm. Its surface is covered with reliefs in the Pipil style. A peculiar gable-like section with smaller, badly weathered reliefs is above the three main human figures. The underside of this large stone monument is also said to be covered by reliefs. I made copies of the visible reliefs, as well as of the small relief at the fountain at El Castillo.

At El Baúl a considerable complex of ruins is located in the middle of bushes and sugarcane plantings, but occasionally large, carefully worked building stones have been carried away. Some of them lie along the private path leading to the highway between the finca and Santa Lucía. One can see three other beautiful building blocks in the vicinity of the sculptured colossal stone head in the approximate center of El Baúl.

Further south and somewhat higher up, some excavations took place some time ago during which a stone block was uncovered that shows a human figure, as well as a Mexican calendar sign in relief. A few paces to the north lies the fragment of a block of granite, covered with weathered Maya decorations. Recently, a stone relief was discovered further west and to the north of a neighboring, surely artificial, hill at about the middle of its base; this stands upright in its pit. I made copies of all these monuments. The last mentioned relief has been photographed by the

Minister Adrián Recinos, although the important hieroglyphic and numerical inscriptions are not clearly visible because a considerable part of the surface has been plastered over. The rubbing copy makes these much clearer. I have baptized this relief "Piedra Herrera."

It is particularly important because we have here a genuine Maya inscription in the middle of the Pipil area. Surprisingly, the inscription starts with a day sign date, followed by four smaller hieroglyphs below in two rows (from the viewer's perspective on the left) followed by additional numbers below. This day sign date could be read as either 12 *kimi* (*miquiztli*) or 12 *eb'* (*malinalli*). My short cycle account done on the spot indicates the latter has to be preferred. The form of the day sign, however, reminds me more of the Mexican than the Maya sign, despite its Maya-type framing of a cartouche. This causes much thought because of its proximity to the old Pipils in Santa Lucía. The cycle inscription itself had apparently been in the first row of the hieroglyphs (left outside) and still belongs to cycle 7. While still in Miramar (Christmas, 1925), I deciphered the date to be 7.19.7.8.12 (4413 x 260 + 212; or 3143 x 365+297—that is, 12 Eb', 20 K'ank'in). Accordingly, the Piedra Herrera would be the oldest of all known Maya inscriptions.

In this connection it is remarkable that I have encountered stelae with Maya inscriptions farther west of Chocolá in the area of Miramar (Colomba). Mr. Max Vollmberg had called my attention to one of them with a letter and sketch some time ago. It is located on the road that leads from the Finca San Isidro Piedra Parada to Retalhuleu. I have made a rubbing of this relief and called it "Piedra Fuentes"; it shows only four small, badly weathered Maya hieroglyphs in a row on the left side (from the viewer's position).

In the adjoining Finca Santa Margarita, another larger stone relief that stood partly exposed above ground was totally excavated with the help of some workers from Schlubach's Finca El Rosario (Bola de Oro). I am calling this relief "Piedra Schlubach." During the excavation a thin layer of dark earth (humus) was removed, after which about two feet of whitish volcanic ash was followed by firm brown earth. The volcanic ash was most likely from the last eruption of the Santa María volcano (about twenty-three years ago). During removal of this firm brown earth a framed cycle inscription appeared in the center of the relief. Unfortunately, the part below, as well as the adjacent figures on both sides, had been destroyed by intentional defacing of the stone surface. The inscription belongs to cycle 7 or 8 but is preserved only at the beginning. In any case, the Piedra Schlubach is an ancient Maya monument. Other cruder stone monuments can be found in the area of the Finca San Isidro Piedra Parada, but none of them shows recognizable traces of hieroglyphs.

During my return from Guatemala to Mexico I spent several days at Tapachula. I succeeded there in recording its language, the Tánitóc, whose relation to the Mixe-Zoque I discussed some time ago in the *Zeitschrift für Ethnologie* (1906). The number of words of the language in Tapachula is quite limited and apparently has been for quite some time, since even very old people could not tell me the word for finger, rabbit, and so on. These are very specific words that are generally missing in that language at this time. At first I thought that the language had totally disappeared, but this is incorrect. It surely will die out in a few more decades, because people are already ashamed of it and the young generation no longer learns it. The vitality of an everyday language among men, and apparently even more so among women conversing with one another, is in the verbs. These are well preserved and richly developed, which my recordings indicate.

I was also able to make word lists of the Maya language from Comitán and Chamula during my stay in Tapachula. The ignorance of the Spanish-speaking population of Tapachula concerning the indigenous Tapachulteco is so great that a teacher

WALTER LEHMANN

told me, for instance, that no special local language exists. Another thought it was the Mam language which now appears to extend only up to Tuxtla Chico.

My trip continued through Soconusco to Tehuantepec. There I found wonderful cool temperatures along with beautiful sunshine on account of the Nortes. Many people speak Zapotec here. However, many Indians from other regions come to Tehuantepec, such as the Mareños from the lagoons, a fishing population with a special language called Huavi by the Zapotecs. These people are fairly timid and speak little Spanish. At the marketplace in Tehuantepec, Zapotec women dominated the individual booths. Only at one corner did I find two Huavi women who were selling *lizas* and *mojarras* (types of fish).

These Huavi women said that they did talk among themselves in their language, but they would not tell it to a stranger. Later I was able to make recordings of the language of the Mareños in their hut shelters and even penetrated into the difficult conjugation. This language is differentiated from others of the region in that it has a dual number for the first, second, and third persons.

In addition to the lagoon fishers from San Mateo del Mar, Chontal speakers from Tequisistlán also come to Tehuantepec. I was also able to make recordings of this peculiar language, as well as of the Zapotec and of a Zapotec dialect from the district of Miahuatlán. The Zapotec is dominated to a large degree by down-steps and is almost incomprehensible without knowledge of them.

Now I have traveled from Tehuantepec to Puerto México and hope to get to Palenque in a few days. I may perhaps mention that I have been nominated an honorary professor of the University of Mexico, as well as a corresponding member of the Sociedad de Geografía e Historia de Guatemala.

NOTES
1. *Talud-tablero* refers to elements of an architectural form. The *talud* is the sloping base; the *tablero* is the vertical paneled plane above the *talud*. The *talud* acts as a base for each *tablero* platform. Usually each *tablero* was decorated with painting or sculpture.
2. "Here" is Puerto Mexico, which is the old name for the town of Coatzacoalcos.
3. We assume this reference is to Ixtacehuatl, the extinct volcano southeast of Mexico City.
4. Consultation with linguists resulted in the tentative definition of *letras heridas* as what currently are called "glottalized consonants."

Bibliography

Bozzoli de Wille, Maria E.

1975   Birth and death in the belief system of the Bribri Indians of Costa Rica. Ph. D. dissertation, University of Georgia. Ann Arbor: University Microfilms.

1979   *El nacimiento y la muerte entre los Bribris.* San Jose: Editorial Universidad de Costa Rica.

Brasseur de Bourbourg, Charles Etienne

1861   *Popul Vuh. Le livre sacré et les mythes de l'antiquité américaine, avec les livres héroĪques et historiques des quichés .* Paris: Collection de documents dan les langues indigènes, pour servir à l'étude de l'histoire de la philologie de Amérique ancienne, 1.

1862   *Grammaire de la langue quiché survie d'un vocabulaire et du drame de Rabinal Achi.* Paris: Collection de documents dan les langues indigénes, pour servir a l'étude de l'histoire de la philologie de Amérique ancienne, 2.

Bray, Warwick

1981   Gold work. In *Between continents between seas. Precolumbian art of Costa Rica,* edited by Elizabeth Benson, 152–166. Detroit and New York: Detroit Institute of the Arts and Harry N. Abrams, Inc.

Brigham, William T.

1887   *Guatemala. Land of the Quetzal.* New York: Charles Scribner's Sons. Facsimile reproduction, Gainesville: Latin American Gateway Series, University of Florida Press, 1965.

Burkitt, Robert

1930   Excavations at Chocolá, Guatemala. *The Museum Journal* 21(1): 4–40.

Burns, E. Bradford

1980   *The poverty of progress: Latin America in the 19th century.* Berkeley: University of California Press.

Burrus, Ernest J., S.J.

1973   Religious chroniclers and historians: A summary with annotated bibliography. In *Handbook of Middle American Indians* 13: *Guide to ethnohistorical sources, part 2,* edited by Howard F. Cline, 138–185. Austin: University of Texas Press.

Cardenal, Ernesto

1979   *Nueva antología poética.* 2d. ed. Mexico: Siglo Veintiuno.

Chinchilla Mazariegos, Oswaldo Fernando

1996a   Settlement patterns and monumental art at a major pre-Columbian polity:

Cotzumalguapa, Guatemala. Ph.D. dissertation, Department of Anthropology, Vanderbilt University, Nashville.

1996b Las esculturas de Pantaleón, Escuintla. *U'tzib* 1(10):1–23. Guatemala City.

1997 Notas sobre los barrigones de Escuintla, Guatemala. Unpublished manuscript.

Comas, Juan

1974 *Cien Años de Congressos Internacionales de Americanistas.* Mexico: Instituto de Investigaciones Historicas and Instituto de Investigaciones Antropológicas.

Day, Jane S.

1988 Golden images in Greater Nicoya. In *Costa Rican art and archaeology. Essays in honor of Frederick R. Mayer,* edited by Frederick W. Lange, 203–211. Boulder: University of Colorado.

Flores, Lazaro, and Wendy Griffin

1991 *Dioses, heroes, y hombres en el mundo mitico Pech.* San Salvador: Universidad Centroamericana.

Fonseca Z., Oscar M., and Richard Scaglion

1978 Stylistic analysis of stone pendants from Las Huacas burial ground, northwestern Costa Rica. *Annals of Carnegie Museum* 47:281–298.

Friederichsen, Ludwig

1876 Carta geográfica de la República de Costa Rica (Centro América). Hamburg and Berlin: Instituto Geográfico de L. Freidrichsen y Co. and Anst. V. Leopold Kraatz.

Fuentes y Guzmán, Francisco Antonio de

1882 *Historia de Guatemala, o Recordación florida, escrita en el siglo XVII...que publica por primera vez con notas e ilustraciones D. Justo Zaragoza.* 2 vols. Madrid: L. Navarro.

1932-33 *Recordación Florida. Discurso historial y demonstración natural, material, militar y politica del Reyno de Guatemala.* Prólogo del Licenciado J. Antonio Villacorta C. Biblioteca

Goathemala, 3 vols. Guatemala: Sociedad de Geografía e Historia.

Gabb, William M.

1876 On the Indian tribes and languages of Costa Rica. *Proceedings of the American Philosophical Society* 14:483–602.

Gibson, Charles

1973 Published collections of documents relating to Middle American ethnohistory. In *Handbook of Middle American Indians 13: Guide to ethnohistorical sources, part 2,* edited by Howard F. Cline, 3–41. Austin: University of Texas Press.

1975 A survey of Middle American prose manuscripts in the native historical tradition. In *Handbook of Middle American Indians 15: Guide to Ethnohistorical Sources, Part 4,* edited by Howard F. Cline, 331–321. Austin: University of Texas Press.

González Chaves, Alfredo and Fernando González Vásquez

1989 *La casa cósmica Talamanqueña y sus simbolismos.* San José: Coedition Editorial de la Universidad de Costa Rica and Editorial Universidad Estatal a Distancia.

Hardy, Ellen T.

1992 The mortuary behavior of Guanacaste/Nicoya: An analysis of Precolumbian social structure. Ph. D. dissertation, Graduate Archaeology Program, University of California, Los Angeles. Ann Arbor: University Microfilms.

Hartman, C.V.

1907 *Archaeological researches on the Pacific Coast of Costa Rica.* Memoirs of the Carnegie Museum 3. Pittsburgh: Carnegie Museum.

Isagoge

1892 *Isagoge histórico apológético...de Guatemala.* Madrid.

1935 *Isagoge histórica apologética...de Guatemala.* Guatemala: Tipografia Nacional.

Jones, Christopher
1986   A ruler in triumph, Chocolá
        monument 1. *Expedition* 28 (3):3–13.
Keable, B. C.
N.D.   *Coffee from grower to consumer.* London: Sir
        Isaac Pitman and Sons, Ltd.
Lange, Frederick W.
1988   Geographical and chronological
        setting. In *Costa Rican art and
        archaeology. Essays in honor of
        Frederick R. Mayer* edited by
        Frederick W. Lange, 1–10. Boulder:
        University of Colorado.
Lanza, Rigoberto de Jesús, Marcio Tulio
        Escobar, Mauren Denise Carías
        Moncada, and Rosa Carminda
        Castellanos
1992   *Los Pech (Payas): Una cultura olvidada.*
        Tegucigalpa, Honduras: Editorial
        Guaymuras.
Las Casas, Bartolomé de
1876   *De único vocationis modo.* Reprinted
        in *Obras completas*, vol. 2, edited by
        Paulo Castaneda Delgado y
        Antonio García del Moral, O.P.
        Madrid: Alianza Editorial, 1988.
1967   *Apologética historia sumaria...*Edición
        preparada por Edmundo O'Gorman,
        con un estudio preliminar, apéndices
        y un índice de materias. 2 vols.
        Mexico City: Universidad Nacional
        Autónoma de Mexico, Instituto de
        Investigaciones Históricas. Serie de
        historiadores y cronistas de Indias, 1.
Lawrence, John W., and Ellen T. Hardy
1982   Excavation of an early Polychrome
        period tomb at Nacascolo. Ms. on
        file, Departamento de Antropología
        e Historia, Museo Nacional de
        Costa Rica.
Lehmann, Walter
1906a   Traditionen der alten Mexikaner:
        Unveröffentlicher Text und
        Original in Nahuatl Sprache mit
        Übersetzung ins Lateinische.
        Zeitschrift für Ethnologie 38:752–760.
        Berlin

1906b   Die Mexikanische Grünsteinfigur
        des Musé Guimet in Paris. *Globus*
        90 (4): 60–61. Braunschweig.
1920   *Zentral–Amerika: Die Sprachen
        Zentral–Amerikas in ihren
        Beziehungen zueinander sowie zu
        Südamerika und Mexico.* 2 vols.
        Berlin: D. Reimer Verlag.
Lothrop, Samuel Kirkland
1933   *Atitlan. An archaeological study of
        ancient remains on the borders of Lake
        Atitlan, Guatemala.* Publication 444
        Washington, D.C.: Carnegie
        Institution.
Maya Atlas
1997   Maya atlas 1997: the struggle to
        preserve Maya land in southern
        Belize compiled by the Maya
        people of Southern Belize, in
        conjunction with the Toledo Maya
        Cultural Council and the Toledo
        Alcaldes Association; with the
        assistance of Indian Law Resource
        Center, Geography Map Group,
        UC Berkeley, and Society for the
        Preservation of Education and
        Research. Berkeley, Ca.; North
        Atlantic Books.
Membreño, Alberto
1897   *Hondureñismos.* 2d ed. Tegucigalpa:
        Tipografía Nacional.
Mendieta, Geronimo de, O. F. M.
1870   *História eclesiástica indiana: obra
        escrita a fines del siglo XVI.* Mexico.
1971   *História eclesiástica indiana: obra
        escrita a fines del siglo XVI.* Facsimile
        of 1870 ed. Mexico City: Porrua.
Milla, José D.
1879   Historia de la América Central
        desde el descubrimiento del país
        por los Españoles (1502) hasta su
        independencia de la España (1821).
        Precedida de una "noticia historica"
        relativa a las naciones que habitan
        la America Central a la llegada de
        los Espanoles. Reprinted in
        Colección "Juan Chapin," vol. II,

book 1, 2d ed. Guatemala: Tipografía Nacional, 1937.

1882 Historia de la America Central desde el descubrimiento del país por los Españoles (1502) hasta su independencia de la España (1821). Precedida de una "noticia historica" relativa a las naciones que habitan la America Central a la llegada de los Españoles. Reprinted in Colección "Juan Chapin," vol. II, book 2, 2nd ed. Guatemala: Tipografía Nacional, 1937.

Navarrete, Martin Fernandez de
1825-37 Colección de los viages descubrimientos que hicieron por mar los Españoles desde fines del siglo XV, con varios documentos inéditos concernientes á la historia de la marina Castellana y de los establecimientos españoles en Indias. 5 vols. Madrid: Imprenta Real. Reprint, with prologue by J. Natalicio Gonzalez, Buenos Aires: Editorial Guarania, 1945.

Norweb, Albert Holden
1964 Ceramic stratigraphy in southwestern Nicaragua. In *Acta, 35th International Congress of Americanists* (Mexico 1962) 1: 557–61.

Oviedo y Valdes, Gonzalo Fernando de
1851-55 *Historia general de las Indias, islas y tierra-firme del mar océano.* Reprinted in Series biblioteca de historiadores de Indias, with prologue by J. Natalicio Gonzalez and notes by Jose Amador de los Rios, 14 vols. Asunción, Paraguay: Editorial Guarania ,1944.

Parsons, Lee Allen
1967-69 Bilbao, Guatemala; an archaeological study of the Pacific coast, Cotzumalhuapa region. Milwaukee Public Museum Publications in anthropology 11-12. Milwaukee: Milwaukee Public Museum.

Pittier de Fábrega, Henri Francois
1898 Die Sprache der Bribri-Indianer in

Costa Rica. *Sitzungsberichte der philosophisch-historischen Klasse der Klaiserlichen 138.* Vienna: Akademie der Wissenschaften.

Ponce, Alonso
1872-73 *Relación breve y verdadera de algunas cosas de las muchas que sucedieron al Padre Fray Alonzo Ponce en las Provincias de la Nueva España...escrita por dos religiosos, sus compañeros.* 2 vols. Madrid: Coleccion de Documentos Inéditos para la historia de España, vols. 57–58.

Recinos, Adrián
1950 *Memorial de Sololá...[and] Titulo de los Señores de Totonicipan. Traducción del original quiché por el P. Dionisio José Cronay: introduccion y notas.* Biblioteca Americana, Serie de Literatura Indígena. Mexico City and Buenos Aires: Fondo de Cultura Económica.

Remesal, Fray Antonio de
1932 *Historia general de las Indias occidentales, y particular de la gobernación de Chiapa y Guatemala.* 2 vols. Biblioteca Goathemala 4–5. Guatemala: Sociedad de Geografia e Historia

1966 *Historia general de las Indias occidentales, y particular de la gobernación de Chiapa y Guatemala. Prologo del licenciado Antonio Batres Jauregui.* 3d ed. Biblioteca Guatemalteca de cultura popular 91–94. Guatemala City: Editorial Jose de Pineda Ibarra.

Rodas, Sergio
1993 Catálogo de los barrigones de Guatemala. *U'tzib* 1(5):1–36. Guatemala City.

Sanborn, Helen J.
1886 *A winter in Central America and Mexico.* Boston: Lee and Shepard.

Sapper, Karl
1895 Die Gebräuche und religiöse Anschauungen der Kekchí-

Indianer: *Internationales Archiv für Ethnographie* 8:195–215. Berlin

1897 *Das nördliche Mittelamerika nebst einem Ausflug nach dem Hochland von Anahuac, Reisen und Studien aus den Jahren 1888-1895.* Braunschweig: Druck und Verlag von Friedrich Vieweg und Sohn.

1902 *Mittelamerikanische Reisen und Studien aus den Jahren 1888 bis 1900.* Braunschweig: Druck und Verlag von Friedrich Viewig und Sohn.

1906 *Título del Barrio de Santa Ana Agosto 14 de 1565. XIV International Congress of Americanists, Stuttgart 1904.* Vol. 2: 373–381, 383–397.

Schultze Jena, Leonhard

1933 *Indiana I, Leben, Glaube und Sprache der Quiché von Guatemala.* Jena: Verlag von Gustav Fischer.

Seler, Eduard

1990-1996 Archaeological results of my first trip to Mexico. In *Collected work in Mesoamerican linguistics and archaeology. English translations of German papers from Gesammelte Abhandlungen zur Americanischen Sprach-und Alterthumskunde made under the supervision of Charles P. Bowditch with slight emanations to volumes IV and V by J.E.S. Thompson,* edited by J.E.S. Thompson and Francis B. Richardson. 5 vols. Culver City, Ca. : Labyrinthos.

Soustelle, Jacques

1935 La Totemisme des Lacandons. *Maya Research* 2:125–144. New York.

Squier, E.G.

1858 *The States of Central America; their geography, topography, climate, commerce, political organization, aborigines, etc., etc., comprising chapters of Honduras, San Salvador, Nicaragua, Costa Rica, Guatemala, Belize, the Bay Islands, the Mosquito Shore, and the Honduras Inter-Oceanic Railway.* New York: Harper & Brothers.

Standley, Paul C., L.O. Williams, and D.N. Gibson

1970–73 *Flora of Guatemala.* Fieldiana-Botany, vol. 24. Chicago: Field Museum of Natural History.

Stone, Doris

1961 *Las tribus talamacaños de Costa Rica.* San Jose: Editorial Antonio Lehmann.

1962 *The Talamancan tribes of Costa Rica.* Papers of the Peabody Museum, Harvard University, vol. 43, no. 2. Cambridge.

1966 Synthesis of lower Central American ethnology. In *Handbook of Middle American Indians 4: Archaeological Frontiers and external connections,* edited by Gordon F. Ekholm and Gordon R. Willey, 209–233. Austin: University of Texas Press.

Termer, Franz

1934 Über Wanderungen indianischer Stämme und Wanderwege in Mittelamerika. In Actas y trabajos científicos del XXV Congreso Internacional de Americanistas I:323–332. Buenos Aires: Imprenta y Casa Editorial CONDI.

1935 Über die Aufgaben der archäologischen Forschung in den Hochländern des nördlichen Mittelamerika. Seville: Reseñas y trabajos científicos del XXVI Congreso Internacional de Americanistas I:255–261. Reprint, Liechtenstein: Kraus Reprint, 1976.

Thiel Bernardo A.

1896 Viajes a varias partes de la República de Costa Rica. Reprinted in series Biblioteca Patria, annotated by H. Pittier, San José, Costa Rica: Imprenta y Liberia Trejos Hermanos,1927.

Thompson, J.E.S.

1948 *An Archaeological reconnaissance in the Cotzumalhuapa Region, Escuintla, Guatemala. Contributions to American*

anthropology and history, vol. 9, no.44
Publication 574, Washington, D.C.:
Carnegie Institution

Torquemada, Fray Juan de
1723   *Monarquía indiana*. Madrid: N.
Rodriquez Franco. Reprinted in
Biblioteca Porrúa, vols. 41–42;
introduction by Miguel León-
Portilla. Mexico, 1969.

Wagner, Regina
1996   *Los Alemanes in Guatemala 1828–
1944*. 2d. ed. Guatemala: Alfanes,
S.A.

Warren, J. Benedict
1973   An introductory survey of secular
writings in the European tradition
on Colonial Middle America, 1503–
1818. In *Handbook of Middle American Indians 13: Guide to ethnohistorical
sources, part 2*, edited by Howard F.
Cline, 42–137. Austin: University of
Texas Press.

Wilk, Richard R. Wilk
1997   *Household Ecology: Economic Change
and Domestic Life among the Kekchi
Maya in Belize*. DeKalb, Ill.: Northern Illinois University Press.

Ximénez, Fray Francisco
1721-22 *Historia de la Provincia de San Vicente de
Chiapa y Guatemala de la Orden de
Predicadores*. Reprinted in *Biblioteca
Goathemala*, 1–3. 3 vols. Guatemala
City: Sociedad de Geografía e
Historia, 1929-31.

Contributors

Marilyn Beaudry-Corbett
Cotsen Institute of Archaeology at UCLA

Christopher Taylor Begley
University of Chicago
Chicago, Illinois

Frederick J. Bove
ISBER, University of California
Santa Barbara, California

Matthew A. Boxt
California State University
Northridge, California

Brian D. Dillon
Consulting Archaeologist
Sepulveda, California

William R. Fowler
Vanderbilt University
Nashville, Tennessee

Ellen T. Hardy
Cotsen Institute of Archaeology at UCLA

Dennis Holt
Quinnipiac College
Hamden, Connecticut

Payson D. Sheets
University of Colorado
Boulder, Colorado

Richard Wilk
Indiana University
Bloomington, Indiana